Help!

I'm Being Followed

What to Do When You've Been Called to Lead

Clinton A. Valley

Autumn House® Publishing
www.autumnhousepublishing.com
A Division of **REVIEW AND HERALD® PUBLISHING**
Since 1861

Published by Autumn House® Publishing, a division of Review and Herald® Publishing, Hagerstown, MD 21741-1119

Bible texts credited to Amplified are from *The Amplified Bible,* Old Testament copyright © 1965, 1987 by the Zondervan Corporation. The *Amplified New Testament* copyright © 1958, 1987 by The Lockman Foundation. Used by permission.

Texts credited to Message are from *The Message.* Copyright © 1993, 1994, 1995, 1996, 2000, 2001, 2002. Used by permission of NavPress Publishing Group.

Scripture quotations marked NASB are from the *New American Standard Bible,* copyright © 1960, 1963, 1968, 1971, 1972, 1973, 1975, 1977, 1994 by The Lockman Foundation. Used by permission.

Texts credited to NEB are from *The New English Bible.* © The Delegates of the Oxford University Press and the Syndics of the Cambridge University Press 1961, 1970. Reprinted by permission.

Texts credited to NIV are from the *Holy Bible, New International Version.* Copyright © 1973, 1978, 1984, International Bible Society. Used by permission of Zondervan Bible Publishers.

Texts credited to NKJV are from the New King James Version. Copyright © 1979, 1980, 1982 by Thomas Nelson, Inc. Used by permission. All rights reserved.

Scripture quotations marked NLT are taken from the *Holy Bible,* New Living Translation, copyright © 1996. Used by permission of Tyndale House Publishers, Inc., Wheaton, Illinois 60189. All rights reserved.

This book was
Edited by Gerald Wheeler
Copyedited by James Cavil
Designed by Ron J. Pride
Cover art by iStockphoto®
Typeset: Bembo 11/14

PRINTED IN U.S.A.
12 11 10 09 08   5 4 3 2 1

Library of Congress Cataloging-in-Publication Data

Valley, Clinton A.
  Help! I'm being followed : what to do when you've been asked to lead / Clinton A. Valley.
     p. cm.
  Includes bibliographical references.
  1. Christian leadership. 2. Leadership—Religious aspects—Christianity. I. Title.
  BV652.1.V35 2007
  253—dc22

                                    2007029179

ISBN 978-0-8127-0461-7

Dedication

To Ula Sylvester Valley,
my mother and first mentor
on the principles of Christian leadership

To order additional copies of *Help! I'm Being Followed,*
by Clinton Valley, **call 1-800-765-6955.**

Visit us at www.reviewandherald.com for information
on other Review and Herald® products.

Dr. Valley conducts leadership workshops and seminars across
the United States and internationally. He may be contacted for
- Speaking appointments
- Worship service or meeting assessment briefings
- Leadership training for administrators, pastors,
  department heads, or lay church officers
- Strategic planning workshops for executive boards
  and governing committees
- Mentoring for Christian leaders

Please contact Dr. Valley at
Walla Walla University
204 S. College Avenue
College Place, WA 99324
509-527-2395
Clinton.calley@wallawalla.edu

Acknowledgments

It's a privilege for me to offer this book on Christian leadership. I am indebted to so many for making this possible that I fear to list any names lest I forget someone. However, I must first give gratitude to my God for His amazing love and grace and for calling me into His service. I have served as a denominational employee for more than 30 years, and I have no regrets in the way in which the Lord has directed my steps. As a family we rejoice in the blessings of the Lord.

Then I give thanks to my family, especially my wife and partner for more than 30 years. Martha has indeed been the choicest of God's blessings in my life, and I give Him the praise for her. Thanks also to our children for their love and for unwittingly providing, along with my wife, an ongoing crucible for the honing of my leadership skills. To my extended family—both biological and spiritual—I offer my thanks for your prayers, your encouragement, and your support through the years. I reserve special thanks for my mother and mentor for her unstinting love and care. Now in the sunset of her days, she is the first and the best Christian leader that I have known. I dedicate this work to her.

I also acknowledge the editorial support so carefully provided by my administrative assistant, Bev Scott. Thanks, Bev, for services above and beyond the call of duty. And thanks to my former university president, Jon Dybdahl, for reading the manuscript and offering valuable feedback.

Contents

Preface 9

Foreword 13

Introduction 17

Chapter 1   Leadership Exposed 19

Chapter 2   You've Been Called! 25

Chapter 3   What Are You Doing Here? 33

Chapter 4   Go for Growth 45

Chapter 5   The Christian Leader's Profile 50

Chapter 6   Christian Leadership—
An Honorable Ambition 59

Chapter 7   The Essence of Effectiveness 68

Chapter 8   A Call to Excellence 78

Chapter 9   The Lone Ranger Is Dead 83

Chapter 10   It's Time for Change 93

Chapter 11   When the Road Gets Bumpy 100

Chapter 12   A Case Study in Christian Leadership . .107

Epilogue 113

Appendix 116

Selected Bibliography 124

 # Preface

This book is about Christian leadership. You have picked it up either because you are a Christian leader or you are interested in the nature of leadership. This work will enhance your knowledge and skills in this fascinating area. While the focus here is on Christian leadership, the principles in it also apply to other leadership settings, because the leadership process is generic to all organizational settings. Leadership is leadership is leadership.

As a Seventh-day Adventist minister and educator, I am thankful to the church for nurturing my leadership potential. I remain ever grateful for the numerous opportunities I have received through the years to grow and develop as a Christian leader. I love my church for what it has done for me and for millions of others who have come to know Jesus and His love as a result of its ministry. Probably we can all testify that we have been able to grow in a variety of ways because of the glorious Advent message. Being passionately committed to our worldwide mission, whatever I write in this book must be understood in that context.

First, let me share my personal experience in the leadership realm. I was born on the Caribbean island of Trinidad. Having grown up as a devout Roman Catholic, I served for a time as an altar boy, the priest's assistant. I committed myself to Christian service at a religious shrine at the age of 12. At 15 I had my first excursion into leadership when a group of us organized ourselves as the Presentation Social Movement—a name chosen because most of us were students of the Roman Catholic Presentation College. Our organization had as its goal relieving suffering and providing hope for people in our community. I would rush off after school to clothing manufacturers to secure their seconds and throwaways to take to people in our local community. While preparing for our own high school final examinations, we also ran evening classes for dropouts, instilling in them new hope and opportunity. Those first experiences in leadership were quite exciting and helped to cement my interest in this field of study and practice.

I became a Seventh-day Adventist Christian at the age of 16 and shortly thereafter went to Caribbean Union College (now University of the Southern Caribbean) to train for the pastoral ministry. For a year I pursued graduate studies in the United States in the fields of church leadership and educational administration before returning to the Caribbean, where I worked as a minister and an educator for the Seventh-day Adventist Church. Sensing the need for further academic preparation, I returned to the United States and completed a doctorate in educational leadership. The program focused on theory building and concept formation in the broad area of leadership, which served me in good stead, for I was able to integrate my study with my professional and spiritual roles as a church leader. After completing my doctoral work, I went to work in England, first as a church pastor, then a departmental director, and then a high school principal and guest lecturer at Newbold College. While in England I completed an MBA at Nottingham University. After returning to the United States in 1999, I served for a time as a pastor in the Atlanta area before joining the administrative team at Walla Walla University as associate academic vice president.

Thus, after 30-plus years in various areas of church leadership, I have decided to delineate some principles and perspectives on Christian leadership that emanate from my study and experience. I share the concern of the leadership of the Seventh-day Adventist Church that effective leaders are one of the critical needs of this expanding organization. If current growth rates continue, the church is expected to have a membership of more than 50 million by 2020. The training of leaders for our churches, schools, and other institutions and organizations is therefore rightly a high priority.

A recent decision by the General Conference of Seventh-day Adventists has also given additional impetus for this book. Meeting in St. Louis, Missouri, in July 2005, the church voted to accept a document on Seventh-day Adventist leadership. The summary of the document in the *Adventist Review* states:

"The Seventh-day Adventist Church is global, a church of great diversity and complexity. Its geographic spread and rapid growth, especially in developing regions of the world, has provided the church with immense richness and opportunities, as well as new challenges. Among these challenges is the need for an increasing number of mission-focused leaders, individuals that are professionally competent, exemplify Bible-based values of Christian leadership, and embrace the expectations for leadership within the worldwide Seventh-day Adventist Church. This need will not be met without a planned process of leadership development of both church employees and laity" (July 14-28, 2005, p. 71).

The document also described the nature of Seventh-day Adventist leadership as follows:

"The Seventh-day Adventist Church affirms the need for leaders with a high level of competence in their fields of leadership. The church values and encourages the development of a range of gifts and desires leaders who have the experience, skills, and qualifications necessary to meet the requirements of the widely disparate leadership positions available throughout the world church. The church is enriched by the professionalism and diverse talents such leaders bring to the church.

"The church also affirms the need for all leaders in the church to share a common commitment to core Christian leadership values that are based on biblical principles, as well as to specific expectations that arise from the theology and global nature of the Seventh-day Adventist Church. This commitment will be evidenced in their approach to their responsibilities and should be a requirement of appointment to any church leadership position" (ibid.).

The document then lists seven major characteristics of Seventh-day Adventist leaders and identifies four main areas for leadership development: curriculum, networking, professional growth, and evaluation. A major goal of this book is to contribute to these objectives.

My hope is that it will be an asset in the continuing leadership training of Christian leaders. We all need to work together for the fulfillment of our church's mission through effective leadership. My background training in the field of leadership has given me the opportunity to include some insights from the literature and practice of leadership today. I am not apologetic for studying and including information and approaches from the secular literature on leadership, for I believe that God gives knowledge to all. We listen to non-Christian doctors, lawyers, educators, and even politicians. After filtering what everyone says through our own spiritual lens, we pick the best and leave the rest. I value my spiritual worldview, and this, under the unction of the Spirit of God, is my benchmark for assessing everything that comes before me. And it is my approach here.

By writing this book, I am not saying that I have all the answers. It simply indicates that I have been in the trenches of leadership and have some scars to show and tell! Please look over my shoulder and review the principles and perspectives discussed. I encourage you, dear reader, to continue to study and practice the fine art of Christian leadership so nobly exemplified in our Master Teacher and Leader, the Lord Jesus Christ.

Foreword

For the Christian leader, life is becoming more complicated every day. Society changes so rapidly that methods to accomplish stated objectives seem to shift just as fast as well. We must always be ready to adapt to circumstances in nurturing God's church and the evangelistic mission He has given us, a concept supported by Scripture and the writings of Ellen White. Clinton A. Valley's book, *Help! I'm Being Followed*, provides you, current or prospective leader, with perspectives and tools to help make you more effective in these last days of earth's history. As we approach the momentous times just ahead predicted by John the revelator and outlined by Ellen G. White, we know that spiritual leaders will be tested to the ultimate degree. It will not be possible to truly lead unless you are connected completely to the Savior. As our ultimate leader, He must be paramount in our thinking and decision-making.

Leadership in the Seventh-day Adventist Church is not summed up in grand honor and popular opinion. It is grounded in complete, selfless service to ideals and principles outlined in Scripture and the Spirit of Prophecy. Although leadership styles may vary because we are different people, a common thread of spiritual commitment will bind our work into one magnificent momentum. It will be not because we are leadership geniuses, but because we are submitted to the Holy Spirit's power to work in us.

Individual approaches and unusual circumstances may produce variations on how to accomplish commonly agreed-upon policies and objectives. However, one thing that should never differ or change is the commitment on the part of Christian leaders always to follow God's leading rather than human tendencies and commonly accepted leadership approaches. Here is where true spiritual Christian leaders will differ greatly from their business or political counterparts. Valley sums it up nicely when he declares, "The standard of success, therefore, is not the deafening hurrahs of the crowd, but faithfulness in fulfilling the will of God."

Although we may not all agree with or feel comfortable with every aspect of Valley's leadership models, that is not what is important. What is vital is realizing his emphasis on the importance of constantly reaching for new ways in which to serve the Lord effectively through true servant leadership—a servant leadership that exemplifies Christ's spiritual and humble approach to motivating and leading His church to accomplish its mission. Valley states that "Christian leadership is servant leadership. It is found in losing oneself in service to others, not in coaxing or inducing others to serve you and your interests."

Reading this book prayerfully will inspire you to become a more visionary and credible spiritual leader. You will find yourself pushed to communicate more effectively and with greater passion for the spiritual objectives of our great Advent movement. To provide for conviction in portraying the role of the servant Christian leader of the twenty-first century, the author draws on biblical references, Spirit of Prophecy resources, counsel from well-known Seventh-day Adventist and other religious leaders, and from his reservoir of personal pastoral and leadership experience. His practical and anecdotal writing approach will encourage you to submit yourself daily to the guidance of the Master Leader, Christ Himself.

As we approach the challenges ahead, we are not to lose hope, not to despair as Christian leaders. Instead, we are to stand ever more firmly on the foundational principles portrayed in Scripture. Do not waver. Do not lose focus on Christ and His power. Do not lessen your emphasis on the prophetic destiny of this Advent movement. God is calling for leaders of unusual ability—the ability to lean on Him through everything and to point God's people to Christ and His soon coming. This is our calling. As Clinton Valley plainly states toward the end of this volume: "Ultimately, Christian leadership is about preparing people for a better, more satisfying life, both now and eternally." May this book help you to do just that and make you a courageous spiritual leader for God's church through the power of the Holy Spirit.

—Ted N. C. Wilson
General Vice President
General Conference of Seventh-day Adventists

"You Have Done a Great Service to All"

Clinton Valley is a credible witness. He speaks from experience: from altar boy to pastor; from the classroom to the boardroom; from conference to college administration—and from the Caribbean to England to the United States. "Been there, seen that, done it!"

More than just interesting, his witness is usable. *Help! I'm Being Followed: What to Do When You've Been Called to Lead* is distilled wisdom. It is not a doctoral dissertation. While it is evident that Valley has read widely, he has gone beyond that. He has lived what he preaches. His concepts have been tested in the crucible of real life. I must say it again: it is usable—not just principles or maxims, but true application. He writes of principles brought to bear on life situations.

Most of all, Valley, a man of erudition, reads the Bible with insight and imagination. He skillfully makes the biblical narrative speak to "my situation." This is priceless. But don't be afraid—he isn't preachy!

There is challenge here also—the faith community must be a model of all this. We must make it visible and believable, and, above all, make it work. We are—every one of us—leaders.

I picked up so much that is usable in my own situation: "A leader works with the compliant and the defiant, the bright stars and lesser mortals, striving to understand them all, to work within the context of their needs and to motivate them to pull together for the sake of the team."

Books aplenty there are on leadership. Valley's is in the "must read" category. You just cannot afford to ignore him!

—Charles Bradford
Retired North American Division president

Introduction

A plethora of studies exists in the field of leadership in general and Christian leadership in particular. The bibliography at the end of this book cites a number of them. I have studied broadly in the field and read many of the works cited, particularly those from the Christian perspective. However, I have attempted here to look at Christian leadership from another faith perspective—that of a Seventh-day Adventist Church leader, minister, and educator. I have adopted the approach of "milking from many cows in the process of making my own butter."

Furthermore, many books on the market today that purport to deal with leadership are actually fine works on management. As Warren Bennis puts it, they emphasize "doing things right" (Warren Bennis, quoted in Cherie Carter-Scott, "The Differences Between Leadership and Management," *Manage*, November 1994, p. 12). On the other hand, the emphasis in this book is on "doing the right thing." We will look further at the distinction between leadership and management later.

My focus is not on "how to" insights and techniques, but rather on the conceptual, spiritual, and theological role of leadership in the Christian church. A paradigm shift in our thinking about leadership is necessary before we begin any consideration of management approaches. Policies, processes, and procedures may all require reexamination as we seek to create a new culture of mission-focused leaders within the context of our theology and prophetic purpose. Visionary, mission-focused leaders will need a flatter hierarchy more willing to take risks than the classical bureaucratic structure allows.

Therefore, we cannot talk about leadership without also discussing organization. It would be futile to create a new cadre of twenty-first-century Christian leaders and ask them to function effectively in an early-twentieth-century organizational structure. If we sense that we need not merely more leaders, but also a new breed of them to address the complex and diverse challenges facing our twenty-first century church, then we must look at the current structure to determine if it is the right vehicle for developing such leaders.

The church is in constant need of leaders. We need them for our churches, schools, hospitals, conferences, unions, divisions, and the General Conference. In addition to our paid employees, the world church depends heavily on a vast army of volunteer leaders to carry forward its global mission. In a broad sense, too, God calls every person to lead, for He has gifted all of us, and we are responsible for the wise use of the talents and resources He has entrusted to our care. Ellen White wrote:

"To His servants Christ commits 'His goods'—something to be put to use for Him. He gives 'to every man his work.' Each has his place in the eternal plan of heaven. Each is to work in cooperation with Christ for the salvation of souls. Not more surely is the place prepared for us in the heavenly mansions than is the special place designated on earth where we are to work for God" (*Christ's Object Lessons*, pp. 326, 327).

We all have been called to lead our lives, our homes, our professions, and our ministries in a manner that pleases God and blesses humanity. For the continuing growth and development of all Christian leaders, I offer this book.

The first two chapters define leadership and illustrate the concept of a spiritual call. Next I look at the purpose of leadership. I focus in chapter 3 on the goal of the leader and in the following chapter on the purpose of organization. Chapters 5 and 6 discuss the profile of the Christian leader, and chapters 7 and 8 review the product or result of Christian leadership. These latter chapters highlight the two important themes of effectiveness and excellence. The next three chapters shift to the other people involved in the leadership process—the followers. Chapter 9 emphasizes the values of team leadership. Chapter 10 deals with the pivotal work of the leader—directing change and overcoming resistance to it in the organization—while chapter 11 suggests ways for dealing with disagreements and conflicts. Finally, in chapter 12 I recount my own most challenging experience in Christian leadership. The appendix contains a series of choice quotations on leadership from Ellen White. I have also provided an extensive bibliography for those who desire further reading.

Leadership Exposed

Corporate America faces a leadership shortage. Four hundred forty-one CEOs left their jobs during the first four months of 2005, according to *Newsweek* (June 13, 2005, pp. 42-46). That was 88 percent higher than for the same period in 2004. Such a skyrocketing rate of executive turnover has fueled talk of crisis in American boardrooms. Institutional boards struggle to fill what were once considered plum jobs as the implications of the leadership train wrecks from Enron, Tyco, MCI, Boeing, and other corporate giants sink in. Such institutional disasters have triggered new legislation and procedures, but rules and regulations do not change the inordinate desire for wealth and power that drives the human heart. The church has a role to play in modeling before the world ethical and effective leadership.

I am therefore delighted that the Seventh-day Adventist Church has voted leadership development as one of its current priorities. So much hangs or falls on leadership. Harris Lee asks the pertinent questions: Why do some churches thrive while others languish? Why are some vital and purposeful while others flounder? He admits that there may be many reasons, but one factor not often discussed is "the leadership factor: the quality, quantity, and timeliness of the leadership exercised by pastors and elected leaders of congregations" (*Effective Church Leadership*, p. 19).

A longstanding tradition assumes that anyone can lead. But it is based on a misunderstanding of what leadership is and its pivotal role in an organization. James MacGregor Burns states that leadership is one of the "least understood phenomena on earth" (*Leadership*, p. 2). Arnold Kurtz, my professor in church leadership and administration at Andrews University, expressed his frustrations over the fact that we do not take just anyone and make them into a scientist, a musician, or a technocrat, yet we attempt to do exactly that in the area of leadership. According to Kurtz, all these roles require a measure of aptitude and preparation. A correct understanding of the leadership phenomenon will help to clarify this misconception.

Leadership—A Process, Not a Person

Let us begin by defining leadership. When we speak of leadership, we are not talking about a person or a group as much as we are discussing a process. We may glibly remark that a team or organization needs leadership, meaning that it requires someone able to function more effectively than the present leader. However, if there are no followers, there can be no leaders. Therefore, what is demanded is someone who can unite the different strengths of the followers and reduce their weaknesses to accomplish the intent of a team or organization. We will therefore use the following as our working definition of leadership:

Leadership is an influence process initiated by a person who harnesses the varied strengths of a group of people and minimizes their weaknesses in a concerted effort to achieve mutually agreed-upon goals.

The concept of initiating has not traditionally been included in the definition of leadership, but I am indebted to Robert Greenleaf for this idea. Greenleaf, a well-known authority on the servant-leader concept, maintains that leadership also initiates, that is, it goes out ahead to show the way. He observes that church leaders settle too much for the maintenance aspects of leadership, but the result is neither a well-served church nor society. To him, leaders serve by initiating (*Servant Leadership*, pp. 44, 45).

Leadership is a system of interaction that involves both a leader and followers within a given context or situation. Thus leadership is the interplay of these elements. We may state it as a formula:

$$L = f (l, f, s)$$

Here L represents the end product of leadership, and l, f, and s stand for leader, follower, and situation (context), respectively. The parentheses and the f—the function sign—indicate the interaction that takes place among the various elements.

Leadership—An Influence Process

The leader influences followers to work together to achieve organizational goals. As Christian leaders today, we face new and exciting challenges. With declining morals, rising levels of assertiveness, lowered commitment to supporting Christian organizations, and an increasing questioning of traditional values, leading a Christian organization is certainly growing more and more difficult. Globalization, urbanization, and rampant materialism add additional complexity to the leadership process. More than ever, leaders need to learn how to influence others to accomplish organizational goals despite ambiguity and rapid change. You may be appointed to lead a college department, a church congregation, or a ministry at the regional or national level, but you really become the leader only when you are able to persuade others to follow you in accomplishing the stated purpose of the organization or institution.

Leading Is Not Managing

Let's clarify the distinction between *leading* and *managing*. You may be appointed to a *management* responsibility, but you assume *leadership* through the process of influence. Earlier literature on leadership made a distinction between the leader's *position power* and *personal power*. In the former, leaders occupied the role because of an appointment or election, while in the latter they earned it through the process of influence. The former is really a manager or administrator, while the latter is a leader. The leader may not necessarily be the one appointed to that role. Rather, he or she provides the significant influence in a given context.

John Kotter explains that modern management came about because of the need to "produce consistent results on key dimensions expected by customers, stockholders, employees and other organizational constituencies." Management was needed "to keep a complex organization on time and on budget." He notes that from his studies, "managerial careers in organizations produce individuals who are remarkably narrow in focus and understanding, moderately risk averse, weak in communication skills, and relatively blind to the values of others. They produce people who know more how to play games with a budget than how to achieve the real achievements of their people" (*A Force for Change*, pp. 119, 120).

Leadership, on the other hand, is very different. It deals with movement and change. The leadership process involves "establishing where a group of people should go, getting them lined up in that direction and committed to movement, and then energizing them to overcome the inevitable obstacles they will encounter along the way" (*ibid.*, pp. 4, 5). Thus "managing" deals with consistency, whereas "leading" involves change.

Warren Bennis highlighted the distinction between leaders and managers in this way:

"The manager administrates; the leader innovates. The manager is a copy; the leader is an original. The manager maintains; the leader develops. The manager focuses on systems and structures; the leader focuses on people. The manager relies on control; the leader inspires trust. The manager has a short-range view; the leader has a long-range perspective. The manager asks how and when; the leader asks what and why. The manager has his eye on the bottom line; the leader has his eye on the horizon. The manager imitates; the leader originates. The manager accepts the status quo; the leader challenges it. . . . Managers do things right; leaders do the right things" (quoted in Carter-Scott).

Leaders begin by asking such questions as: Where does this organization need to go? What needs to be done? What can I do to move it along to accomplishing its mission? Leaders look to the organization's mission and goals to determine their role and what counts as success in that organization.

Many churches, colleges, and institutions are overmanaged and underled. Our organizations need management, but they also need to be led. We require both for an effective organization. Rick Warren explains that when we have only management in the church, we get the problem of paralysis of analysis. "It's like 'Ready . . . Aim . . . Aim . . . Aim . . . ' And they never fire" (*Ministry Toolbox*, Aug. 3, 2005). We witness this when we see committees established because of a fear to take an action. Many good ideas get killed simply by being sent to a committttee. Management without leadership results in constantly analyzing and looking, but never actually doing anything. On the other hand, if we have only leaders without managers, we may end up with an organization that operates "Ready . . . Fire!" without ever taking the time to aim. We need both!

Successful and Effective Leadership

The terms *successful* and *effective* have been used interchangeably in discussions of leaders, but successful and effective leadership is not the same. Success concentrates on short-term results, while effectiveness focuses on long-term impact. Thus success deals with

- quick production
- completing the program
- operating by "any means possible"
- getting the "milk" at all costs

On the other hand, effectiveness seeks
- lasting productivity

- to achieve the desired effect
- to operate from deeply held principles
- to also care for the "cow"

Some years ago I had the distinct pleasure of visiting with Charles Handy, one of the foremost leadership theorists in England. I was part of a group of leaders in the public realm in London who spent the morning with Handy in what he described as a "Socratic session." We discussed four questions, the first of which was What is success and how do we measure it? Handy spent considerable time exploring the difference between success and effectiveness, or results and impact. He called one *first-order success*, while the second he referred to as *second-order success*. First-order success brings the cameras in, gets the accolades, evokes the applause, and facilitates the promotions. Second-order success, on the other hand, deals with the usually unnoticed long-term implications. I remember Handy pointing to me, then a high school principal, and explaining, "Your first-order success is your students' end of high school results" (in England students at the end of high school sit for the national GCSE examinations, and the results for all schools get published in the national league tables). "But," Handy continued, "your second-order success is whether these students have been developed as thinkers, whether they have learned the discipline of study" (Seminar on Leadership in the Public Realm: A Socratic Session With Charles Handy, Oct. 3, 1997).

Given the visible and personally gratifying benefits of first-order success, is it any wonder that some leaders focus so much more on it, maybe even trying to manufacture it by putting a spin on reality to create the desired perception? The bottom-line mentality has taken over our culture. Why did so many of the 441 CEOs leave their jobs during the first four months of 2005? I suspect that the demand for quick results would have been a major factor. Athletic coaches get hired and fired based on the level of the performances of their teams. University presidents experience similar fates. In our organization we measure effectiveness by bottom line indicators such as attendance figures, baptisms, budgets, student FTEs, occupancy rates, or various other ratios. Long-term impact hardly ever features in our considerations.

We hear of evangelists who hurry ill-prepared baptismal candidates into the water to get the numbers right. Treasurers and accountants delay payments on invoices to obtain acceptable end-of-month statements. Teachers and professors drill their students to score highly on tests rather than teaching them to critically analyze and process data. And school, conference, or institutional administrators magnify the positives and minimize the negatives regarding issues of their stewardship. It is the game people play because society generally places a higher priority on first-order success.

But effective Christian leaders operate from a different set of principles. Our goal is life transformation. It is to foster "a life-changing experience," to borrow the published aim of Walla Walla University. The standard of success, therefore, is not the deafening hurrahs of the crowd, but faithfulness in fulfilling the will of God. That is not to say that first-order success is not important. We do expect leaders to deliver results, but they should not be short-term quick fixes at the expense of the long-term health of the organization. Yes, effective leaders still get the "milk," but they do so while also caring for the "cow." They see themselves as faithful stewards of God's "cow" (the organization). We all do well to heed 1 Corinthians 4:2: "It is required in stewards, that a man be found faithful." We will discuss this further in the next chapter when we look at the call to Christian service.

"Lord, I care not for riches,
　Neither silver nor gold;
　I would make sure of heaven,
　I would enter the fold;
　In the book of Thy kingdom,
　With its pages so fair,
　Tell me, Jesus, my Savior,
　Is my name written there?"
　　　　　—Frank M. Davis

QUESTIONS FOR DISCUSSION

1. **Do you agree with the definition of leadership** presented in this chapter? If not, Why?

2. **Do you see yourself as a leader,** a manager, or one of the followers?

3. **What changes does your church** or organization need to make in the way it evaluates programs in order to place greater emphasis on long-term effectiveness rather than short-term successes?

You've Been Called!

Introduction

By the year 2020 the Seventh-day Adventist Church anticipates that its membership will reach about 50 million members. Such burgeoning growth will create a significant demand for leaders for the additional congregations, schools, hospitals, conferences, unions, and the increased support staff of the General Conference and all its divisions. Apart from the paid employees, the world church depends heavily on a vast army of volunteer leaders to carry forward its global mission. In a broad sense, too, every person is called to lead, for all have been endowed with gifts from God and are therefore responsible for the wise use of the resources entrusted to their care.

The document adopted at the St. Louis General Conference session called for "an increasing number of mission-focused leaders, individuals that are professionally competent, exemplify Bible-based values of Christian leadership, and embrace the expectations for leadership within the world-wide Seventh-day Adventist Church." But what's unique and different about Seventh-day Adventist Christian leadership?

First of all, unlike corporate America, a leader in God's church is "called," rather than appointed. The word "call" has a special meaning, for it denotes a spiritual source. It is true that denominational service begins with possibly a telephone call from the chair of a search committee, a nominating committee, or a conference official. A letter from the organization or a vote by the local congregation may follow it up. But beyond these actions of committees and individuals, every opportunity for service ultimately comes from God. Indeed, every Christian has a life summons to some area of ministry. As Henry and Richard Blackaby state in their book *Spiritual Leadership*: "Spiritual leadership is not an occupation: it is a calling. Christian businesspeople, physicians, educators, politicians, and parents—

all ought to be spiritual leaders" (p. xi). Every one of us has a God-given responsibility to lead.

As a fellow church leader, I share in the many challenges and frustrations of church employees in fulfilling our responsibility to Christian leadership. We struggle with:

- failure to achieve desired goals and objectives
- lack of commitment on the part of many followers and associates
- criticisms from those we are seeking to help
- thorny and often unsolvable department, church, or institutional problems that sap our time and our energies
- family pressures—pleas for our time and our interest
- internal pressures for personal growth and for acceptance and affirmation

It's not easy being a leader, especially a Christian leader. The wind blows the strongest at the top of the mountain, and we live with the reality that a leader's failure has a greater negative impact on the organization than that of a follower. But if God has commissioned us to lead, we can be assured that He will be at our side to guarantee our success. Whomever He calls He qualifies, sustains, and protects.

Next, I want to suggest that three core characteristics lie at the heart of effective Christian leadership. To illustrate them, I want to draw our attention to a little-known Old Testament leader: Micaiah. We read about him in 2 Chronicles 18.

Let me first give the background. King Ahab wanted to go to war against Syria at Ramoth-gilead, but needed the help of Jehoshaphat, the king of Judah. So he arranged a summit meeting, and in the midst of the food and the fun, he made the request. Jehoshaphat, being a godly king, reminded him of the need to seek counsel from the Lord. So Ahab hastily assembled his 400 prophets and had them tell him what he wanted to hear. Since they were Ahab's employees, it became a case of he who paid the piper calling the tune. Leaders are in a dangerous place when they surround themselves only with yes men and women. It is better to be criticized by a wise enemy than to be praised by a not-so-wise friend.

Ahab's prophets held the title, performed the rites, engaged in the symbolisms, and exhibited the trappings of power, but they were just paid pipers. They played whatever tune Ahab wanted to hear. As a result they were of little real help to him when the crunch came.

What then are the three core characteristics of one called by God to lead? First, we must be:

Fervent in Our Commitment

Micaiah, a simple, ordinary man, could boast of no wealth or fame, no privileged birth or heritage—he was simply Micaiah, the son of Imlah. He surfaces on the biblical stage in a mere two chapters, and they are but separate accounts of the same event. But God had summoned Micaiah to the prophetic office, and he took his call seriously. Thus he affirmed, "I saw the Lord sitting upon his throne" (2 Chron. 18:18). When encouraged by the servant to agree with what the other 400 prophets were saying, Micaiah's simple response was "I can tell him only what my God says" (verse 13, NIV). It reminds me of a prayer, classic in its brevity and poignancy, that Bobby Richardson, former New York Yankees second baseman, offered at a meeting of the Fellowship of Christian Athletes. He prayed: "Dear God, Your will, nothing more, nothing less, nothing else. Amen." That's Micaiah's spirit. And that should be our spirit as well.

Commitment is not a popular word today. We live in a transient culture, a throwaway society. Because everything seems to be temporary, commitment to any ideal seems passé. The roofing contractor for our new church building in Atlanta assured me that he gives a lifetime guarantee on his roofs. How long was that "lifetime," I inquired. No more than 20 years, he replied. Sounds like a dog's lifetime!

One man, clearly lacking in marital commitment, found himself hauled by his wife into a marriage counselor's office. As soon as they sat down, she began to rant about her frustrations, talking faster than the speed limit in the state of Idaho. The counselor listened for a while and then suddenly got up, reached over to the woman, and gave her a warm, tender, passionate kiss. She stopped, obviously in shock, while her husband looked on in stunned silence. Then the counselor spoke to the husband.

"This is what your wife needs—at least twice a week."

The man thought for a moment, then replied, "OK. I'll have her here on Tuesday and Thursday afternoons!"

Fervent commitment does not come by accident. It is the result of a daily walk with the Lord, of spending time with Him, and of seeing Him sitting on His throne. The depth of our commitment reflects the strength of our relationship with our Lord. Amid the din of our varied human activities, purposeful and beneficial as they are, we must pause to catch a fresh glimpse of God. Let us not be so immersed in the work of the Lord that we forget the Lord of the work. Our prayer ought to be "Lord, free us from the endless routine of classes, committees, meetings, and visits, as well as the many plans and programs and projects that we wish to take on; free us, Lord, from making these mundane pursuits such priorities in our lives that our commitment to You is no longer first and foremost." We are to stand strong and true to our commitment no matter which way the wind blows!

Faithful to Our Calling

The second essential characteristic for effective Christian leadership is to be faithful to our calling. Micaiah was thrust in prison by the same Ahab who was now requesting his services. It would have been so easy for the prophet to have indulged in bitterness and revenge and refused to get involved. He could have reasoned that his situation couldn't get any worse, so let Ahab do whatever he wanted. Of course, such an attitude is destructive to both the person and the organization that individual serves. Micaiah was determined that nothing—absolutely nothing—must interfere with his divine calling to declare the will of God. The Lord had chosen him to be a prophet, and he was going to fulfill his call. Regardless of the circumstances, he was going to do his job.

Some teacher or administrator may have hurt you, some church members may have been unkind, or the conference may not have given you the consideration you think you deserve, but none of these are valid reasons for leaving the church, quitting your position, or doing as little as possible in your classroom or office. We have to keep human issues separate from our divine call. Difficulties at home or at work must not translate into a problem with our God. Nothing and no one must ever curb our zeal, dilute our commitment, or stifle our passion to faithfully fulfill our divine call. Human beings may disappoint us, the organization's directions may raise questions within us, but I rejoice that our God never fails us.

But Micaiah's faithfulness angered Zedekiah, the chief of the state prophets. Zedekiah had a vested interest in keeping Ahab happy whether doing so was in the king's best interest or not. Ahab wanted to go to war, so Zedekiah sent the word through the ranks that it was what the monarch wanted to hear. The word to Micaiah therefore was "Don't rock the boat!" When Micaiah told the king the truth, Zedekiah reacted by slapping him (verse 23).

Zedekiah typifies all those who are more concerned with maintaining a self-serving bureaucracy, doing what is politically correct rather than advancing the cause of truth. He also had the attitude held by many church leaders today: "I am the leader. Either do it my way or hit the highway!" If you took church office or are in church employment for the pomp and prestige it provides, for the attention you receive, for the power you control, or for any other earthly factor, you are apt to react defensively, as Zedekiah did, when anyone or anything threatens your position or status.

The danger always faces us that we may become so tied to our organization, to our well-oiled machinery, to our rich heritage, to our lovely church structures and services, that we forget the reason for their existence. We could become so protective of what we have that we are unwilling to risk, to change, or to advance if such actions are necessary to further the kingdom of God. But we are a people of mission. Let not the bright lights of popular acceptance and success blind us from humbly and faithfully doing God's will.

J. R. Sizoo reminds us: "Let it never be forgotten that glamour is not greatness; applause is not fame; prominence is not eminence. The man of the hour is not apt to be the man of the ages. A stone may sparkle, but that does not make it a diamond; people may have money, but that does not make them a success.

"It is what the unimportant people do that really counts and determines the course of history. The greatest forces in the universe are never spectacular. Summer showers are more effective than hurricanes, but they get no publicity. The world would soon die but for the fidelity, loyalty, and consecration of those whose names are unhonored and unsung" (*Bits & Pieces*, June 22, 1995, p. 11).

What has God called you to do and to be for Him? Are you faithful to that calling today?

Fearless of the Consequences

Finally, one summoned to lead in God's work faithfully serves regardless of the consequences. The scene in which Micaiah had to present the Lord's message was one to strike fear in a lesser mortal. At the gates of Samaria sat Ahab and Jehoshaphat on their thrones, arrayed in royal robes. Immediately encircling them were the 400 prophets and the respective armies attending both kings.

Yet Micaiah did not flinch. He would not phrase his words to please the king, to guarantee his future, or to be in accord with all the prophets. His concern was fulfilling the will of God, not seeking human honor. He was not going to play the game of political correctness. Fearlessly he presented the message the Lord gave him. Because it angered Ahab, the king sent him to prison. Yet the voice of the man of God contained no remorse, bitterness, or anger. He spoke the truth and left the consequences with God.

Nelson Mandela spent decades in prison for his stance against apartheid. Sentenced in the Rivonia trial of 1964 and facing the death sentence, he could still declare:

"I have fought against white domination, and I have fought against black domination. I have cherished the ideal of a democratic and free society in which all persons live together in harmony and with equal opportunities. It is an ideal which I hope to live for and to achieve. But if need be, it is an ideal for which I am prepared to die" (Pretoria Supreme Court, Apr. 20, 1964; www.anc.org.za/ancdocs/history/rivonia.html).

People today tend to be results-oriented. We weigh every action and decide whether to speak or to remain silent based on what might promote our future. James McGregor Burns in his classic work *Leadership* refers to this as transactional leadership, for it is based on a psychological exchange. I weigh what I say by what it does for me in return. In contrast, Burns talks about the transformational leader who speaks and acts from conviction without reference to personal benefit. Here is the Christian leader's imperative. I do or say what is right because it is right, and I leave the consequences with God. While I need to exercise Christian grace and tact, I must not flinch from speaking or living truth for fear of my personal welfare.

Of course, I must add that not all fearless acts spring from deep convictions. One village chief decided that he wanted the bravest and most fearless man in his village to marry his daughter. The prospective son-in-law would also receive up to half of the chief's wealth. Calling all the men together around a large pool containing an alligator, he announced that any man who swam the pool in spite of the creature would have his daughter's hand in marriage and up to half of his wealth. For a while nothing happened, and then suddenly eyes turned in the direction of a man, fully clothed, swimming across the pool at breathtaking speed. Eluding the alligator's every attempt to get to him, he safely made it to the other end and scampered out of the water. As the crowd applauded, the local chief rushed up and declared that he could marry his daughter.

"No," the man said. "With due respect, chief, I do not wish your daughter's hand in marriage."

Surprised, the chief said, "Well, you can have up to half of my wealth."

"No," the man insisted. "I do not want any of your money."

Even more surprised, the chief asked, "Then why did you swim across the pool? What do you want?"

"Sir, I just want to find that fool who pushed me into the water!"

Why do you do what you do? Is it because of fear, fame, or the favor of your Lord?

Conclusion

King Ahab did go to battle against Syria, but the enemy soundly defeated his army. Even though Ahab disguised himself, a stray arrow got him, and he died that evening. Meanwhile Micaiah remained in his prison cell. Scripture does not record that he was ever acknowledged or rewarded for his message. But for the Christian leader, it really does not matter. Instead, we do right because it is right, and not with the hope of any rewards. Nor do we let either applause or censure influence us.

We need more leaders like Micaiah. He could have lived in palatial comfort and been part of the king's entourage. All he had to do was not rock the boat. But he remained true to his God. Is there a price tag on your commitment? Would you trade it for popularity, for power, or for special perks? Micaiah never walked the halls of power and influence. The Holy Word leaves him on the way to his prison cell. Yet even then his concern was not for himself but for the truth. "Take heed" were his last words to the people.

Such unwavering commitment, such unyielding faithfulness to his call, such unconcern about consequences, is what genuine Christian leadership is all about. That's the kind of leadership our world and our church desperately needs. Our role is to faithfully do what we are called to do and then leave our future with God. That future may be in some distant pastorate or in a sought-after presidency; in a multigrade classroom or a modern lecture hall; in the executive suite or in the basement heat; on the top floor or on the shop floor. Wherever we are, we must serve with conviction no matter what. Ultimately we seek divine, not human, approval. Doubtless Ellen White had such leaders in mind when she wrote:

"The greatest want of the world is the want of men—men who will not be bought or sold, men who in their inmost souls are true and honest, men who do not fear to call sin by its right name, men whose conscience is as true to duty as the needle to the pole, men who will stand for the right though the heavens fall" (*Education,* p. 57).

· Jesus is the supreme model for Christian leaders. From the womb to the tomb He lived to bless others. From the cradle to the cross He was focused on His calling. He said: "My meat is to do the will of him that sent me, and to finish his work" (John 4:34). Even when unjustly sentenced to a Roman cross, He stopped dying long enough, not to rescue Himself, but to save a converted thief and to pray to His Father: "Father, forgive them; for they know not what they do" (Luke 23:34). I encourage you today to lead like Micaiah, and indeed like Jesus. Be fervent in your commitment, be faithful to your calling, and be fearless of the consequences.

QUESTIONS FOR DISCUSSION

1. If you were in Micaiah's position, would you have acted the way he did? If not, what would you have done differently? How would you feel about having to express an unpopular minority viewpoint? Do you think Micaiah had any second thoughts about the way he dealt with the situation?

2. Is the prophet's approach relevant today, or do we need to be more subtle or accommodating?

3. King Ahab didn't want to hear any opinions that differed from his. Do you or does your leader face a similar challenge? Are you or your organization threatened by an alternative viewpoint?

What Are You Doing Here?

Introduction

Elijah had done great things for God. He had stood against 450 false prophets at Mount Carmel and uplifted the name and power of the Almighty. After thoroughly defeating the false prophets, Elijah was riding the crest of spiritual success.

But Jezebel had other plans. She decided that she was going to destroy the prophet. And so Elijah ran for his life. Angels first found him under a juniper tree in a terribly frightened state. There he received some food and then ran like crazy. We find him in 1 Kings 19 at the entrance of a cave. Here the word of the Lord came to him in verse 9: "What are you doing here, Elijah?" (NIV).

What are you doing here? Where's your focus? Where's your faith? Where's your sense of mission? My son, my church leader, why are you here in this pitiable condition? Who's your God? Isn't He the same God who worked miracles on Mount Carmel? Has He lost His power to deliver and save? How come you are scared of one woman?

Elijah responded with a litany of woes. He said in verse 10 that he had been zealous for the Lord, but the children of Israel had forsaken the covenant, thrown down the altars, and slain the prophets. "I am the only one left, and now they are trying to kill me too" (NIV). Poor Elijah! The church is split, sin is rampant, all the other pastors have been run out of town, and I am the only one left!

It must have pained God's heart to listen to Elijah's diatribe. Someone who had accomplished tremendous exploits for Him was now bellyaching in a cave, scared to death. Discouragement is a terrible affliction that can happen to any Christian leader. The moment we lose our hold on the Lord and begin to feel that it is "all of me and none of Christ," we become the target for the enemy. Faith gives way to fear; courage succumbs to cowardice; and daring collapses into discouragement. Such was Elijah's predicament at the entrance of the cave. A religious leader without any plan for tomorrow, he simply huddled there waiting for the inevitable. It sounds strangely familiar to many Christians today and, indeed, to many Christian leaders and Christian congregations. The question is valid for all of God's current Elijahs: What are you doing here?

Our loving Lord chose to give the prophet another glimpse of His power. Elijah needed reminding that he served the God of heaven and earth. And so God sent a mighty wind, so powerful that it shattered rocks on the mountain. Then the Lord disturbed the earth's foundations and caused a mighty earthquake. A great fire swiftly followed. Finally God spoke in a still small voice. Once again the question came: What are you doing here, Elijah?

One would have expected that the fresh glimpses of God's glory would have stirred faith in him. Remember, he was not a new member in the church, but a godly leader of great experience. Unfortunately, even fresh revelations of divine power did not move him. When we lose our spiritual connections, we take divine blessings for granted or just regard them as chance occurrences. Instead of standing in church giving testimonies and singing, "The Lord is blessing me right now," we find ourselves sighing, "I was lucky—it just happened that way!" But nothing "just happens"! We must ever recognize the hand of God in our affairs.

But to Elijah, the divine visitation made no difference. When asked the same question again, he gave the identical response (verse 14). It seems as if Elijah had programmed himself to respond in this way. Many congregations and many individual Christians also seem to operate in a similar manner. Their responses do not arise from a living, active relationship with the Lord, but rather from a learned or traditional response. Our church services, our testimony sessions, and our prayers sometimes betray the absence of an active relationship with the Lord as we descend into mouthing hackneyed and overworked expressions. Christian leaders may continue to maintain the rites and responsibilities of their sacred offices, conducting meetings, leading committees, counseling colleagues, teaching classes, attending to patients, and presenting messages from the pulpit—all without a sense of the awesome God for whom they labor. The earthen vessel may continue to impress, but the divine unction is absent! Elijah's experience is a classic case of form replacing faith, of religiosity substituting for rightdoing, of the work of God taking priority over the God of the work.

Our Lord challenged Elijah to go back and get involved once again in the work he loved. We are happiest when we feel fulfilled in what we do. Those of us at Walla Walla University rejoiced when former president Jon Dybdahl returned to the helm after a yearlong medical leave. Jon was quite prepared to surrender the reins of leadership if he felt so impressed and his family and colleagues so desired, but with support and encouragement from all he reassumed the mantle, declaring, "There is fire in the belly again!" Making a difference—doing what you love—is medicine to the body as well as to the mind.

God told Elijah, "The best cure for your discouragement is to get back to doing what you love. Go appoint Hazael to be king of Syria, Jehu king of Israel, and Elisha to be your successor as prophet" (see verses 15, 16). Faith develops through its exercise. Social scientists tell us that behaviors influence beliefs. Thus the Lord sought to resurrect Elijah's faith by getting him involved in the divine enterprise. Go back to your first love. Retrace those memorable faith experiences. Witness and do exploits for God. The best way to develop as a swimmer is to keep on swimming! So God challenged Elijah to leave his cave and get back to work.

The question posed to the prophet also applies to us today: What are you doing here, Christian leader? Like Elijah, many Christian leaders and congregations today are battle-weary. Many sit by figurative juniper trees or caves, sullenly complaining, "I only am left!" For many, faith is absent, witnessing is nonexistent, lives are purposeless, Christian love is a thing of the past, and many are either dead spiritually or just waiting to exhale.

Some leaders moan and groan about other leaders and recount all the pains and hurts they have suffered at their hands. In the process they spread discouragement with their constant bellyaching. Some seek their leader's demise at the next constituency session. If they fail in their attempt, they then spend the ensuing four or five years planning for the next opportunity. Thus they waste the time between constituency sessions merely waiting and grumbling! In their churches and classrooms routine has become the order of the day. Their service has no life-giving power, for their hearts are not in it. As a consequence, their churches and schools suffer from a lack of inspiring leadership.

I remember attending a particular church one day. My wife and I and our two children arrived at the entrance and were immediately taken aback by the huge, thick, closed wooden double doors that towered 10 feet over us. It was our first visit to this congregation, and we did not know what to expect.

Gingerly we opened the doors and were relieved to enter a foyer area. But it was empty, and ahead of us stood another pair of imposing wooden doors. Again we summoned the courage to open the doors, and saw two groups of worshippers in the main sanctuary studying the Bible lesson for that morning. Slipping into the back of one of the classes, we nodded a greeting to the one conducting it. During the remaining 25 minutes of the discussion we received no acknowledgment of our presence. As visitors to the church we were not welcomed, offered a hymnal, or given any gesture of appreciation for our presence. The first words spoken to us came at the end of the break period when the local leader inquired if I was the preacher for the day. When I replied in the affirmative, he solemnly instructed me to follow him.

Throughout the service I had a distinct impression that the congregation had slid into mere form and routine. The poor believers meant well, but Jesus could have entered that church service and they would not have known it! Leader, what are you doing here?

Neither churches nor individuals have to be like that congregation. We are here to live purposefully and as God intended. To do this, we must have a connection with God. In Acts 2 we find an example of a congregation that was focused on its reason for being. Here were people who knew what they ought to be doing and went about their Father's business. We will highlight three salient features of this New Testament congregation as a model for the refocusing and revitalization of purposeless leaders and churches today. If we are to fulfill God's plans for us, then we must be connected to Him and the rest of His creation through worship and fellowship, and we must have a clear sense of our mission.

Worship

Acts 2:41 recounts the establishment of the New Testament church with the addition of 3,000 individuals. We immediately notice that their worship life was something special. They devoted themselves to the apostles' teaching (Bible study), participated in prayer (verse 42), attended the Temple daily, witnessed from house to house (verse 46), and praised God (verse 47).

Clearly this church took its worship life seriously. It did not compromise with sin or sinners. You can't give light if you are not shining! Sometimes in an effort to be politically correct, leaders are afraid to take needed actions to preserve church standards, weakening them as a result. But the leaders of the New Testament church did what was necessary while at the same time maintaining an atmosphere that was warm and filled with prayer and praise.

Christian leaders should seek to model the spirit of praise and thankfulness in every situation. Our lives ought to radiate the glow of heaven. In my years in pastoral ministry I have tried to avoid late meetings or events on Friday evenings if I were speaking the following day. The preacher needs to be fresh, alert, and hopeful when standing in the pulpit. Tired preachers who slouch in the pulpit and just go through the motions won't communicate faith to their congregations.

I remember sitting in a small congregation one Sabbath morning and listening to a leading church official deliver the morning message. He leaned against the pulpit, his face bearing the effects of a stressful week. Repeatedly he spoke of problems in the local conference. Suddenly an elderly woman blurted out, "Pastor, you are talking so much about the problems. Do you know the Problem-solver?" She made the statement with such force, yet with such simplicity of faith and trust, that we were all stunned! Of course, the speaker had a difficult time recovering from that comment and regaining the attention of his audience.

Some people you dare not ask how they are. They are so negative that they would immediately subject you to a diatribe of woes and injustices done to them that leaves you feeling jaded and downcast. Yet we must learn to praise God anyhow. "In every thing give thanks: for this is the will of God in Christ Jesus concerning you" (1 Thess. 5:18). Instead of moaning and groaning to others who cannot help us, we need to experience again the power of prayer. Leaders must lead in prayer. Prayer is the opening of the heart to God as to a friend. The key difference is that God *can* help us. We need to talk less of our woes and pray more concerning them. And we must speak less of the problems and more of the power of God to solve all problems.

Sometimes we have more trust in technology, human expertise, and our well-laid plans than we do God. One colleague at a meeting of ministers said he was shocked to receive a cool response when he called for a moment of prayer in the midst of a difficult and seemingly unresolvable situation. We run the risk of utter dismay and total discouragement if we seek to live our lives, lead others, or manage organizations apart from God's will and power. To keep trusting and smiling either in the sunshine or the storms of life, we must have Christ both at the center and circumference of our lives.

Threats to Corporate Worship Today

1. No Private Devotional Life. Two major threats face our church worship today. The first is the absence of a private devotional life. Members are so busy that they find little or no time to maintain a personal walk with their Lord. The stresses of raising a family, holding down two jobs, planning for holidays, and so forth tend to crowd God out of our reckoning. Many treat church like a service station that they come to for a quick fill for the week. They arrive as late as possible and leave as early as they can because their agendas are so crowded. Some are like the young man who said nightly as he slumped into bed, "Same as usual, Lord!" As Christian leaders we need to guard our devotional life. Members, meetings, manuscripts, or the multitude of other tasks that daily come our way must not crowd out the time that we need to nurture our own spirituality. We cannot give what we do not have.

Once Christians studied their Bibles fervently and took pride in committing large portions of Scripture to memory. It was beneficial not only spiritually but also academically. Educators have long attested to the positive values of memorization. But the spiritually dead in church now want the preacher to do for them what they failed to do throughout the week. As a result, many find church boring and stay away. For them, it has become a needless routine, a disposable extra. But how can we live for God if we do not hear from Him through prayer, study, and worship?

The place where dead people congregate is a cemetery. Many churches are nothing but spiritual cemeteries. It takes live coals to ignite a fire. When individual members walk with Christ during the week, they come burning with testimonies to share, and their singing and worshipping give evidence of their relationship with Him. A meaningful worship service results from the celebratory coming together of a happy, joyous, spiritually alive people who have lived with and for their Lord during the past week. What am I doing here? Well, I am here to praise the Lord!

2. Fear of Change. As Christian leaders, we need to periodically inject our routine activities with new life. The absence of planning means that we do this year just as we did last year, the year before, 10 years ago, or even 50 years ago! We must continue to examine our programs and practices. Yesterday's ways, methods, people, and ideas may not be appropriate to the challenges of tomorrow's problems and people. While core principles do not change, practices and policies need to, if the church is to remain relevant in a changing society. From a critical analysis of the status quo, let us adjust the routine, disturb the beleaguered format, and remain open and responsive to the Spirit's leading.

I was in the vestry of a church one morning with five local elders, preparing for the worship service. The head elder, seeking to engage in some light conversation, made it known to me that they were all very experienced elders. Four of them had served for more than 30 years. Looking at the drab surroundings and the dullness of the first service, I mentally noted that these leaders didn't seem to make a significant difference to the vitality of the congregation. Observing that the head elder did not refer to the fifth leader, I pressed him as to how long this elder had served. "Oh," the head elder replied, "he just came. He has only been an elder for about 12 years!" In that congregation I saw many who just sat and listened to the service, apparently going through the motions of a religious rite that had little or no relevance to their real lives outside the church.

J. Oswald Sanders points out that too many Christian leaders cling to positions long after they should have passed them on to younger people. He refers to one leader who was in his 90s but was still the superintendent of his congregation's Sunday school. Young people were willing and available, but no one in the church had the courage to talk to this saint about retirement. And so he continued on, blocking opportunities for younger, more energetic individuals and frustrating many in the process (*Spiritual Leadership*, p. 157).

Of course, the issue of senior leaders not passing on the torch to younger ones is not limited to the local congregation. At all levels and areas of the organization we find a general reluctance to surrender the mantle of leadership when it is clear that age has blunted one's energy and performance level. One former conference president in England remarked that once you've been a president, you live in fear of becoming an "un-president." Thus you just keep seeking another term! It may be helpful to generalize the idea of a two-term limit for executive appointments.

What imprisons us in sameness is, of course, the fear of change. Those five elders and that superintendent had always been the leaders and, by inference, should always remain so. Someone has said that the seven last words of the church are "We have always done it this way." The expression seeks to end all discussion and stifle any change. But if worship is to be meaningful, it must arise from the current experiences of the members as they live out their Christianity through the week. While strongly advocating order and decency in worship, we must also be aware that worship is our offering of praise and should spring from our daily journey with the Lord.

At the corporate level, we need to be planning for relevance within our community. How can we be significant as a church or a college in our local environment? How can we reach various social and economic classes with our ministries and services? What role can we play in addressing the felt needs of our community? Randy Roberts, pastor of the Loma Linda University Seventh-day Adventist Church, in addressing his congregation after the Hurricane Katrina disaster, advised his members not to tell the people of New Orleans that God loved them. Rather, he counseled, show them! It was a call for relevance.

Our message and mission must have immediate significance to the needs of the university research triangle community in Raleigh-Durham, North Carolina, or to a farming community in Los Bajos, Trinidad, or to young bustling, hustling metropolitan go-getters in Johannesburg, South Africa. To continue to be relevant means that the organization must be prepared to change from time to time. Such change is not an enemy but a friend, and, if managed well, can bring rich dividends to your organization. Church leaders at the local, regional, or national level must all strive to ensure that their organizations remain germane and mission-driven in the midst of a changing society. We just can't continue unquestioningly to do business the way we did it 10, 20, 50, or 100 years ago.

Fellowship

Acts 2 also tells us that the church members had a strong sense of community. They continued in fellowship (verse 42), meeting together constantly and having all things in common (verse 44). In fact, they would sell their possessions and give to those in need (verse 45). This is really amazing stuff! There were more than 3,000 people from different languages, cultures, and backgrounds, yet they were all bound together! Look at the distance our modern church has traveled from the New Testament model.

It is easy for people to assemble for worship. It was such a joyous privilege to attend the General Conference session of the Seventh-day Adventist Church in St. Louis, Missouri. More than 40,000 Seventh-day Adventist believers from around the world gathered there for the final worship services. The parade of nations was a wonder to behold. Members from literally every language, culture, and background celebrated together in the grand finale to a marvelous time of fellowship and unity.

But to reproduce such unity on an ongoing basis in our local communities remains a challenge. As a graduate ministerial student at Andrews

University during the 1970s, I stopped at a gas station in a small town one Sabbath morning to ask for directions to the Seventh-day Adventist church. The attendant, who obviously knew the area well, inquired, "Are you looking for the Black one or the White one?" We still have segregated conferences and segregated churches in the same city. Some unfortunate comments I overheard at the St. Louis General Conference session from both sides of the color line painfully reminded me that we still have a long way to go.

Obviously a long history lies behind these present realities, and the answer is not simply for one group to dissolve and become second-class citizens of the other one. Les Pollard addressed the issue of "what to do with difference" in his presentation on diversity in the Profiling Adventist Leadership lectures at the same General Conference session. He looked to Paul as a model for intercultural awareness and ministry. Pollard asserted that Paul retreats from the racial and ethnic idolatry that could only divide and alienate. His intimate experience as a Jew enables him to be "as" a Jew. Paul works for his own ethnic group, but only as an ambassador from another kingdom (2 Cor. 5:20). The apostle adapted himself to the customs of the Jewish people when working among them. For example, he took a Nazirite vow (Acts 18:18), had Timothy circumcised (Acts 16:3), participated in purification rituals, and paid Nazirite expenses for the sacrificial offering (Acts 21:23ff.). His ministry was Jewish-led but not Jewish-limited. But Paul can also be as one "without the Law," that is, a Gentile. During his times with Gentiles he did not enforce Jewish ceremonial ritual upon them (Gal. 2:11-14; Col. 2:11, 16). Here Paul lays out the possibility for cross-cultural ministry. While he will work for his "own" Jewish people, he refuses to be restricted to them. Rather, he extends his ministry to all people alienated from Jesus Christ. Their diversity represents his opportunity to stretch himself, to move beyond his own comfort zone, to love as Christ loved.

Every Christian leader needs to model this Pauline approach to the diverse people groups that make up the global church family. We serve a God who loves and accepts Brown, Yellow, Black, and White all as His children. As part of our development of new, mission-focused leaders for our diverse and complex world membership, we will need to wrestle with these challenges to fellowship and witness. "That they all may be one" (John 17:21) is still the prayer of our Lord for His people. Pollard's presentation is well worth reading.

Of course, unity does not mean uniformity, nor does it allow for one believer to look up or down at another. One striking feature of the General Conference was the thousands of members who came from England, the Caribbean, Central and South America, and Asia and Africa just to witness the proceedings and to fellowship with other believers. One did not sense a similar passion for fellowship from North America. Thank God for the New Testament model! It calls us to shake off our snobbish indifference and see every person as a child of God and thus a spiritual brother or a sister. He or she may not look like me or talk like me, but we can fellowship together, for they are spiritual siblings and a vital part of the worldwide family of God.

International singing evangelist and my seminarian colleague Wintley Phipps tells the following story. After one of his performances before a large audience in a major U.S. city, an elderly woman enraptured by his music rushed up to him and blurted out, "Pastor Phipps, you blessed my heart! When I get to heaven, I must come over to the Black section to hear you sing!"

The New Testament church was united in fellowship! The ugly specter of racism that still blights us and divides us as Christians will not be present in heaven. In spite of sermons, sensitivity awareness training, and major race summits, we still have a long way to go down here to begin living as God intends—seeing every man or woman as a precious fellow human being for whom Christ died.

As we come closer to Christ, we inevitably approach each other. The church, therefore, must rediscover its role as a caring community. It is a place of acceptance and affirmation—a therapeutic community that heals the hurts suffered from a godless world. Bruised, battered, and buffeted by the devil and his wily agents, members must be able to enter this church fellowship and feel at home—at one with God and with fellow believers. Regrettably, people in some congregations continue the blistering, hurting experiences, and thus provide no relief from the pains engendered from living the week in a cold, unfriendly world.

Thank God, though, other congregations do provide a caring community. I will never forget the Couva Seventh-day Adventist Church in Trinidad, which I joined at the age of 16. The members rallied to my support and helped me to grow, not only spiritually but also physically and emotionally. I had so many Sabbath dinner invitations that I needed a diary to keep track of them all. (The youth today would use their PDA.)

Let me tell you about Sister Williams. I don't remember why I missed the church service one week, but the following week she asked the reason for my absence. Not having a good reason, I lied. "I had no money for the bus fare," I said, thinking that would satisfy her and she would walk away. Well, it didn't! Digging into her huge bag that seemed to carry much of her earthly possessions, she pulled out two $1 bills. "Take that for your bus fare next week," she said, forcing them into my hand. Guiltily I pocketed the money, knowing that I had received it under false pretenses.

But that wasn't the end of it! For several months afterward she would find me without fail after every church service, greet me with a warm smile and a handclasp, and place several dollar bills in my hand for my next week's bus fare. A number of times I tried to evade her, but she was better than the Patriot defense missile: she always found her target! That's what the caring fellowship among Christians should be like.

Mission

The members in that New Testament congregation enjoyed their walk with the Lord and kept an open-door policy for new believers. The baptismal pools were regularly in use. "The Lord added to the church daily those who were being saved" (verse 47, NKJV). Are our churches a welcoming community? If not, what improvements or changes do we need to make to let visitors and members know that they are valued in our congregations?

Sometimes, quite unintentionally, we become so involved with the regulars that we neglect the strangers in our midst. Many visitors to new congregations have complained that the members talked and laughed with one another and left them alone. Take time for the visitors in our midst. Are they comfortably seated? Do they have a program bulletin, hymnal, or Bible? Do they have a place for dinner after the service? Even as the visiting speaker, on many occasions I had to travel several hours to return home after a speaking engagement. No one bothered to think that the speaker might appreciate a meal after church!

Similarly, Christian colleges, universities, hospitals, and all our other institutions need to focus on customer service. Too many in academia have assumed that the students need us, so we do not have to concern ourselves with how we treat them. But this image is changing. While we must be known for our good academics, our parents and students must see Jesus in our lives and on the campuses we lead. The care and attention that we give to people even in the little things say more about the God we serve than our proclivity for research and scholarship. Our hospitals also must have patient care as their first priority as they focus on mission rather than money.

The New Testament church's preaching and teaching were congruent with its lifestyle. What believers preached they lived, and what they lived they preached. Their witness therefore had great power, for it was relevant and demonstrated on a daily basis. Their testimonies were not about a dusty theoretical Jesus, but about one who dwelled in their hearts. That which they saw and heard, and that which they personally experienced, they declared to others. Such living and such witnessing have amazing power!

The Bible reminds us that God is not willing that any should perish. He wants all to be saved. The Christian message is a global one, and every Christian and every congregation or institution is a growth cell for God's kingdom. Christian leadership must facilitate this growth process. Our challenge is to lead people from sin to holiness, from death to life, and from a hopeless end to endless hope in Christ. That's why we are here as leaders!

Acts 2 therefore provides the universal response that congregations and Christian leaders should have in answer to life's most fundamental question: What are you doing here? The Christian, individually and corporately, is to be involved in worship, fellowship, and mission—"up-reach, in-reach, and outreach." All life emanates from God, and we are to be constantly reaching *up* to Him through prayer and devotion and pausing to listen to His Spirit talking to us and guiding us. The need to develop and nurture positive and wholesome relationships with fellow participants of the faith community poses the *in*-reach challenge. Finally, whatever our calling, the mandate to make disciples of all men and women, introducing them to Christ and encouraging them by precept and example to live in harmony with the Christian lifestyle, is our *outreach* mission through all our life's activities. *This* is what we ought to be doing here.

QUESTIONS FOR DISCUSSION

1. Do you have a walk with God or experience with Him? Is there a difference?

2. Is supreme allegiance to God's will pivotal in your or your organization's decision-making?

3. Is your organization a warm, accepting, and Christlike place for visitors? for customers? for employees? What strategies could you adopt during the next year to improve in this area?

Go for Growth

Growth and development is the undisputed mission of every Christian and every Christian organization. The message of the Gospels, the exploits of the book of Acts, the testimony of its author that "the Lord added to the church daily such as should be saved" (Acts 2:47), and the divine mandate of our Lord to "go ye into all the world" to preach and baptize (Mark 16:15)—all point toward a life of growth for the Christian and the Christian organization. Jesus alluded to this concept of growth for all His children in the parable of the tenants in Luke 20. Referring to Himself as the owner and humanity as His farmers, He said: "A man planted a vineyard, rented it to some farmers and went away for a long time. At harvest time he sent a servant to the tenants so they would give him some of the fruit of the vineyard" (verses 9, 10, NIV). The heavenly owner expects fruit from the labors of His followers.

Church growth theorists normally refer to three types of church growth. They are:

- quantitative or conversion growth
- biological growth or the accession of children of members
- qualitative growth or maturation in the spirituality of the individual members

All three areas of church growth are vitally important, and Christian leaders should consider all three in planning an all-round ministry for their department or organization. Qualitative growth is a necessary precursor to quantitative growth. But if quantitative growth ceases, the church begins to die, both spiritually and numerically. Some defend a low growth rate by arguing that they are into quality—not quantity. But they are not opposites. The church needs quality in quantity.

In *Understanding Church Growth* Donald McGavran, widely regarded as the dean of church growth, argues that we demonstrate faithfulness to God through "church multiplication" (p. 22). Ellen White stated that "the church is God's appointed agency for the salvation of men. It was organized for service, and its mission is to carry the gospel to the world" (*The Acts of the Apostles,* p. 9). Of course, an emphasis on the making of disciples and not merely the gaining of snap decisions must undergird this perspective.

The college or university president, the hospital CEO, the institutional head, must all be interested in growth and development. What indicators tell whether your organization is viable and healthy? Do they show that you are a productive leader of the organization? Again, the concern must be not merely the right numbers being reflected but the overall impact of your leadership being one that makes a positive difference.

What makes an organization grow? Obviously, the first answer must be the presence and power of God and His Holy Spirit. No discussion on the subject can proceed without first establishing this spiritual base.

But from a human perspective, according to Peter Wagner of Fuller Theological Seminary's Church Growth Department, the first vital sign of a growing church is a pastor who is a "possibility thinker and whose dynamic leadership has been used to catalyze the entire church into action for growth" (*Your Church Can Grow,* p. 57). Wagner candidly states that many churches are not growing, because their pastor does not labor for growth. He further explains that growth demands a price from the pastor, and many pastors are unwilling to pay that price. The presence of hardworking pastors willing to motivate their members and personally lead them in fulfilling the divine mission characterizes such expanding congregations. Such clergy plan and organize their churches around growth.

This concept of possibility or entrepreneurial thinking lies at the core of organizational growth. Leaders who head up Christian schools, colleges, hospitals, and other institutions also need to share that same spirit. Regrettably, many of us have not been trained to see ourselves as possibility thinkers or growth agents. The traditional clergyperson's responsibilities are mainly maintenance—blessing the babies, marrying the couples, and burying the dead. In short, a hatch, match, and dispatch ministry! Many of our other denominational leaders also seem to be more concerned that the system does not break on their watch rather than seizing the moment and making a significant difference for their organization.

Let me hasten to add that I intend this not as an indictment of leaders but as a statement from observation. The reality is that while most Christian leaders are committed, teachable, and eager to see progress, they lack the background for effective leadership. Some do not have training, others don't possess the aptitude, while yet others simply lack passion. Such leaders cannot give what they do not have. In my own research on church leadership I found that training for the Adventist ministry emphasizes theological content significantly more than the leadership process. The recent emphasis on leadership development is therefore very good news for our church.

As a church pastor, I saw myself as the growth agent in a community of several hundred thousand, not simply the pastor of 300 members. In other words, the focus must be an external one, and the members of the congregation are the pastor's assistants in, rather than the focus of, his or her ministry. This is not to exclude the nurturing functions of ministry, but priority must go to evangelism. All followers need to understand that their leaders should not spend their time attending meetings and hovering over them, but should concentrate on growth opportunities. Referring to the pastor, Mrs. White counsels:

"The best medicine you can give the church is not preaching or sermonizing, but planning work for them. If set to work, the despondent would soon forget their despondency, the weak would become strong, the ignorant intelligent, and all would be prepared to present the truth as it is in Jesus. They would find an unfailing helper in Him who has promised to save all who come unto Him" (*Review and Herald*, June 25, 1895).

Of course, wise leaders know that they cannot do it all themselves. In fact, their effectiveness is in getting the organizational mission accomplished through the coordinated efforts of others. Maximizing the potential of all is the goal, because God has given every person gifts, and they must be encouraged to utilize them fully in His service. The challenge of leaders is to help followers discover their gifts and abilities and then train and empower them for effective service and ministry.

In the congregational setting some could pass out literature and share Bible lessons with friends and family. Home study groups could provide friendly environments for the presentation of truth. We need to explore greater use of the media in spreading the gospel. The satellite television programs and the launch of the Hope Channel are very positive initiatives for our church. Media broadcasting is expensive, but it is a worthwhile investment that pays rich dividends both in building goodwill for the church and in attracting new believers.

In Numbers 13 and 14 we read about Israel in the wilderness. It was time for them to conquer the land and enter the future that God had promised them. But they had armies to conquer, and most of their spies brought back a discouraging report of the fortified cities and the descendants of Anak, who appeared to be giants in the land. Ten of the 12 spies confessed that they were in their own sight as grasshoppers. Those spies suffered from a terrible inferiority complex! *The New Shorter Oxford English Dictionary* describes a complex as a "related group of usually repressed ideas, attitudes, and desires causing a mental or behavioural abnormality." It's a distorted view of reality, yet people act from it.

These 10 spies saw themselves as grasshoppers, and thought leads to action: "As [a man] thinks in his heart, so is he" (Prov. 23:7, NKJV). Whatever the mind conceives, the person believes and the life achieves. Nothing gets accomplished that someone did not first believe to be possible. Every vision is a mental creation before it becomes a physical reality. Thus when these spies said it was not possible to conquer the land, a depressing mood overtook the encampment. Caleb and Joshua tried to introduce another perspective, but the overwhelming fear silenced their voices.

We have such grasshopper mentalities in our committees, our boards, and our business meetings. They are known for saying "It can't be done." Their negativism paralyzes their organizations with inertia and indecisiveness. "The new idea is doomed to fail" underlies their message. The grasshopper spirit exaggerates problems and minimizes God's power. Thankfully, this group is a minority, although at times a rather vocal one.

In contrast to the fear complex of the grasshopper, Caleb and Joshua demonstrated a faith complex. They believed that they were well able to overcome opposition in the name of the Lord. We can do it! they urged. Victory is possible!

As a consequence of the 10 spies' negative report, a journey that was to last a mere 40 days ended up taking 40 years. Forty years of wanderings, frustrations, fights, and failures—all because of the grasshopper complex! God wants the enterprise you lead to move forward—to grow from strength to strength. In this undertaking, you are to embrace all people and all talents. But above all avoid the grasshopper complex. Faith must replace fear and confidence overtake doubt. Believe that the power of God will rule over the forces of evil. Step out of your comfort zone. Go out on a limb for God. Like children who jump trustingly into their daddies' arms, leap forward, believing that "with God all things are possible" (Matt. 19:26).

An entrepreneurial spirit, under the ministry of the Spirit of God, has kept the Seventh-day Adventist Church growing through the years. The establishment of congregations, conferences, schools, hospitals, broadcast ministries, and other institutions all contain a common element of risk-taking and ignoring the naysayers who claim that it can't be done. For instance, H.M.S. Richards, Sr., a Seventh-day Adventist evangelist, pioneered the use of radio to present the gospel from as early as 1929, when many of his colleagues thought the new device was "the devil's tool" (*H.M.S. Richards: Man Alive!*). But he was the forerunner of the church's current global radio and television ministry.

Yes, fellow Christian leader, it *can* be done! Your church and ministry can flourish. Your institution can develop. Pray for it, plan for it, organize for it, and, under God, labor to achieve it.

QUESTIONS FOR DISCUSSION

1. Do you believe that your congregation or Christian organization needs to grow? Why or why not?

2. In what areas should you or your organization be growing from where you are at present?

3. List three targets for growth for you and/or your organization. What resources will it take to achieve those targets? What changes and/or decisions must you make to have them happen?

5

The Christian Leader's Profile

Introduction

A call to Christian leadership is a special honor. In fact, there exists no higher honor on earth than that of being a leader in God's work. In 1 Timothy 3 Paul provides an excellent profile of the effective Christian leader. Let's look at the seven qualities highlighted there.

1. A Holy Desire (verse 1). Paul's revolutionary concept may startle some. We will discuss it in depth in the next chapter, but let us here affirm the apostle's emphasis on a holy and honorable desire as the starting point for Christian leadership. A notion has developed in some Christian circles that positions should go only to those who demonstrate little or no interest in them. Some see it as a sign of spirituality to deny any desire for a particular office or ministry. But why should any organization entrust a responsibility to someone who displays no interest or, worse yet, publicly disavows any interest?

If leaders lack such a holy desire, is it any wonder, then, that many ministries in our congregations and conferences are languishing? That some occupy offices but the offices do not occupy much of their attention? That pastors, despite being employed for years, still find difficulty in giving proof of their ministerial call? Or that the performance of too many teachers and professors cause their employers to hope for their departure? Leaders get out of their ministry what they put into it. In order to prosper, every organization must have leaders who have the interest of God's cause closer to their hearts than any concerns for worldly power, popularity, or pecuniary benefit.

Many valiant church employees around the world do work sacrificially to advance the gospel and hasten our Lord's return. They faithfully teach their classes, lead their committees or departments, chair their boards, attend to their patients, and perform a myriad of tasks for the organization for which they work, simply out of a love for the cause. Betty Duncan, director of academic advisement at Walla Walla University, aptly typifies that spirit. She never says no to a challenge and will devote untold hours to doing what she loves—serving students—without a hint of complaint. We affectionately call her the "mother of advising" at Walla Walla University.

But although we have many who are passionate about their calling, we also have a minority of employees and volunteers whom we ought to feel some concern about. We have full-time denominational employees who spend their best energies selling cars, prepaid insurance, and real estate. Others manage businesses in their spouse's names or seem to have much more vacation time than policy allows. At the local church level, a nominating committee may replace unproductive volunteers. Traditionally, however, church employers have been reluctant to deal decisively with those not fully on task. The holy desire for Christian service will manifest itself in employees who are not clock-watchers but give more, not less, than that required.

2. Morally Upright (verses 2, 3, 7): The Christian leader is to be a moral exemplar. There is no better way to lead in the church, or even in the business world, than by personal example. True leaders will practice what they preach and possess what they profess. As Paul says: "Be ye followers of me, even as I also am of Christ" (1 Cor. 11:1). Such leaders seek to model rather than dictate. But a leader must be a person worth imitating, for character is more easily caught than taught.

An important value for any leader is personal integrity. But moral transparency and openness to scrutiny are especially vital to the effectiveness of a Christian leader. In an age when public figures continue to fail and disappoint, when even Christian leaders get forced out of office because of their less than stellar conduct, and when the cynicism of our times makes anything that is doubtful seem dirty, church leaders need to uphold the highest standards of personal conduct in all personal and professional affairs.

It is a good practice to keep a safe distance from all questionable issues involving money or sex. A leader's lifestyle must be Christ-style. From his research on Christian leaders, George Barna has found that people are willing to forgive a leader who makes mistakes because of still-developing abilities, but will quickly abandon those with declining morals and ethics (*A Fish Out of Water*, p. xxxii).

Truthfulness is another core value for the leader. Politicians are known for their ability to say what an audience wishes to hear, which may or may not accord with the truth. They are also liable to make contradictory assertions to different audiences. Christian leaders do not have that luxury. They should not be saying one thing to one person and something else to another. The members must be confident that what the first elder, the pastor, or the president says is the truth, the whole truth, and nothing but the truth.

Regrettably, it has not always been the case. I have seen occasions when for political expediency, to ensure a particular vote, or to stifle a potential competitor, statements were made and actions taken that were not truthful. Conscientious persons sometimes find themselves unintentionally participating in such situations. Even though they may later apologize to hapless victims, the damage is already done. It is true that the church is an organization, and as such, some of the chicanery of business organizations appears at times. But the church is also the body of Christ; and when one member of the body hurts another, the whole body suffers!

3. *Socially Inviting* (verses 2, 3): Paul teaches that the Christian leader would be patient and given to hospitality. We should expect a positive, hopeful, sunny countenance in anyone called to lead our schools, hospitals, churches, and conferences. Jesus had an alluring personality. He was nice to be near. Leaders, too, should look at the bright sides of issues and keep their confidence even in the most difficult situations. Moody, temperamental leaders will find their effectiveness severely curtailed. Learn to smile. By words and gestures, say to others, "I welcome and appreciate you for who you are."

Being hospitable also incorporates the notion of being willing to inconvenience yourself to make others comfortable. Sometimes it may mean opening up your home, car, or schedule to accommodate a person in need, perhaps someone who can never return the favor. It's easy to take time for professional associates and persons who one day can also "scratch our backs." But it's another story to care genuinely for the "little people" around us, knowing that we are doing good simply for its own sake.

Romans 12:13 exhorts us to contribute to the needs of the saints by practicing hospitality. Hebrews 13:2 tells us that in ministering to strangers some have entertained angels without even knowing it. Servant leaders understand that all they own is to be under the authority of Jesus Christ and is to be used to lift up Jesus and bless humanity.

4. *Professionally Prepared* (verses 2, 6): Paul indicates that the Christian leader will be "apt to teach" and should not be a novice (verse 6). The decision to place a person in a particular office is a serious one that we should

not enter lightly or without prayer. Because leaders greatly influence the departments or organizations they lead, mistakes can be costly. A person's professional preparation is an important determinant in assigning them an office. While all leaders should be forever learning, we should ask someone to lead only if we are convicted that he or she has truly something to offer.

The age at which individuals enter a particular office is not as significant as their preparation. Advanced years do not of themselves confer wisdom, nor does youth necessarily mean inexperience. I am thankful that my small rural church in Couva, Trinidad, invited me to be an elder-in-training at the age of 17. Their vote of confidence heightened my desire for the pastoral ministry. We shouldn't be afraid to give opportunities to the youth but should lead them gently into the water so that they may be able to swim and survive. Leaders must be ever willing to train and trust other leaders for the work of the kingdom.

The Bible teaches that a church leader serves as an overseer. Acts 20:28 says: "Be on guard for yourselves and for all the flock, among which the Holy Spirit has made you overseers, to shepherd the church of God which He purchased with His own blood" (NASB). This word in the Greek is *episkopos,* which means "to care for, shepherd, and oversee." Actually the New Testament uses a number of words to refer to an elder. They include:

- elder
- bishop
- presbyter
- overseer
- shepherd
- pastor

In a broader sense, however, all those called to Christian service, whether in a church, school, or hospital, have similar obligations to be prepared for their roles and to continue to grow. We never reach the point at which we know it all. I once admitted to an elder that I do not have all the answers and still struggle with some issues. His smug, patronizing response was "Pastor, you are still struggling? I am not. Even though I am walking on earth, I am living in heaven." At that point he did not seem to remember that I had been asked to come to his home to provide counseling!

5. Monetarily Disinterested: An inordinate craving for money is one of the two most challenging temptations for church leaders. (Illicit love relationships are the second.) When combined, they especially become a potent force that leads many along the path of personal, professional, and even spiritual ruin. "The love of money," Scripture declares, "is the root of all evil" (1 Tim. 6:10). Money is to be used and wisely managed, but when the desire for it is so strong that a person compromises health, family, friendships, service opportunities, or values, the leader must reconsider his or her position.

It is true that salaries of denominational employees are not what many would like. Many ministerial homes in North America require two incomes to balance the budget and provide for the rainy day. But we must not forget that the Lord promises special blessings. The promises of Malachi are true and available to any trusting, believing servant of God. I have seen and heard many wonderful testimonies of how God has provided and blessed lives. Clothes that last, bodies that remain in health, fun but inexpensive family vacations, home values that appreciate significantly, cars that keep on running long after their "sell-by date," donors who have tangibly expressed their love—all are blessings I have heard of or personally witnessed. Listen to Jesus in Matthew 6: "For your heavenly Father knows that you need all these things. But seek first the kingdom of God and His righteousness, and all these things shall be added to you" (verses 32, 33, NKJV).

Christian leader, the Lord expects you to be wise and prudent in your fiscal management. An old saying reminds us, "Do not hang your hat where your hands cannot reach!" In other words, live within your budget. As Matthew enjoins, when we seek the Lord and He gives us His peace, we do not have to strive to keep up with the Joneses in order to feel OK about ourselves. We may seek what is best for us and our families, but not at the risk of our Christian influence.

Most important, every Christian leader should tithe. If you can speak of your faith in God but can't give Him one dollar for every nine that you keep for yourself, then there is a disconnection between faith and action. If a person will not submit his or her own finances to the will of God, what right does that individual have to exercise authority over the money of the church? Sometimes people who don't tithe are the most vocal as to how we should spend church funds! Judas's problems began because of a love for money. He helped himself to the treasury funds. Every time we keep what belongs to God, we are acting like Judas. Jesus put it this way: "No servant can serve two masters: for either he will hate the one, and love the other; or else he will hold to the one, and despise the other" (Luke 16:13). You cannot serve both God and money.

6. Managerially Competent: Paul considers home management as evidence of the managerial skills of the leader. As we saw in chapter 1, effective leaders must also have management skills. Someone asked former British prime minister Margaret Thatcher early in her tenure about her ability to oversee the British economy. Her response was that she was a housewife, and running the British economy was nothing more than good housekeeping.

Paul suggests that in seeking Christian leaders, we should consider how they function in their homes. We will want to see a well-ordered and managed household. For leaders with families, we will expect to find a home in which the children receive firm yet kind discipline. Spouses and children should regard potential leaders with love and respect. Overall, in the management of the home, in the conduct of personal and business affairs, and in interpersonal relationships, leaders will give evidence of a wise use of time and a commitment to honor their word, to fulfill their promises, and to be transparent in their dealings. Thus they show that they have the qualities to manage the affairs of the Christian organization. "For if a man does not know how to rule his own house, how will he take care of the church of God?" (1 Tim. 3:5, NKJV).

7. *Spiritually Mature:* A potential leader is expected to be a committed Christian. One cannot provide Christian leadership without a personal experience of God's forgiving, saving grace. Since we are talking about *Christian* leadership, being a Christian is really a sine qua non for the position. Prayer, Bible study, and spiritual reflection should be part of the daily practices of the Christian leader.

But spiritual maturity goes further than spiritual commitment. It also allows one to face the storms that come to those in leadership while still retaining dignity and Christian behavior and belief. As we said before, the wind blows fiercest at the top of the mountain, and those leaders not settled in Christ may lose their hold on Him when buffeted by the strong winds of doubt, dissension, and difficult decision-making. Leadership carries with it a measure of loneliness, sometimes amid great uncertainties. Such times demand a close, living relationship with the Lord.

Paul also stressed how important it is for the leader not to be a novice—"not a new convert" (verse 6, NASB). And he explains why: "So that he will not become conceited and fall into the condemnation incurred by the devil" (verse 6, NASB). God knew we would be tempted to elect people because of their looks, their speech, their social rank, or their family ties and connections rather than because of their spiritual preparedness.

Samuel almost made the same mistake when he wanted to anoint one of David's good-looking brothers as king. It is dangerous to push spiritual babes into adult roles. They will be of little use, can become conceited, and perhaps can even lose their own souls. Using secular criteria in selecting leaders can lead us inadvertently to rush unprepared people into office while keeping out qualified, better prepared candidates.

Scripture admonishes all believers to study the word of God so that they can become effective dispensers of it: "a worker who does not need to be ashamed, rightly dividing the word of truth" (2 Tim. 2:15, NKJV). When people seek advice, they need to hear what the Word of God says about a situation. People must sense from talking with you, from listening to your counsel, from hearing your testimony, and from seeing your faith that they are in the presence of a spiritual leader.

Christian churches, schools, hospitals, and other religious organizations have a right to expect that their leaders will model Jesus Christ in their relationships. I have heard of elders who have physically attacked pastors over disagreements! A colleague once remarked that some leaders are so quarrelsome that if we left one of them in a room alone, he or she would argue with himself or herself. I once had an elder walk up to the platform to challenge my leadership during a church service. The Christian leader should be a peacemaker instead of a troublemaker.

Another valid expectation in a Christian environment is that leaders will protect their followers' confidences and privacy. When told something in confidence, an effective leader for Christ does not pass it on in the guise of a prayer request for someone else. We should never use this mechanism to gossip or to destroy the reputation of others. To violate the confidence of anyone is to betray the call of Christ to love one another.

Bear in mind that while not all those you work with will act as Christians, the call to obedience and Christian love remains the same. No Christian organization can afford leaders who are ready to give someone "a piece of their mind." If people tried to make life hard for Jesus and to upset Him, why should His servants expect to fare any better? If you are not willing to suffer pain, disappointment, and injury to your pride, you're not ready to be a Christian leader.

It never ceases to amaze me how hurt and offended some leaders become when they don't get reelected. Both in the local church and in conference leadership at all levels, we see bitterness from some not returned to office. Even though the church assigns positions just for set periods, the widespread feeling exists that once we are in, we must always be in. Perhaps our appointment to that office caused hurt to another person, but we felt justified because it was "what the people wanted." What's different when it's my turn to exit? Often some claim that it's not what was done so much as how it was done. Granted, not all our decision-making processes have been fully Christlike, but a spiritually mature Christian looks beyond the procedures and sees the final outcome as the will of God. Having served on several nominating committees, I know that despite the wills of various persons and factions, the Spirit of God still remains in charge of the church. I am therefore convinced that the decisions that finally emanate are what the Lord allows at that time.

As Christian leaders we must believe that while men and women may plan and plot, ultimately God remains in control. A tree is best measured, not when it's towering in the sunny, blue sky, but when cut down to the ground. Anybody can pray and praise when all is well, but the mature Christian continues to do so even in the midst of a crisis. We can hear the spiritual maturity of Paul as he commented on what was probably more than just his physical circumstances in Philippians 4:12, 13:

"I know how to be abased and live humbly in straitened circumstances, and I know also how to enjoy plenty and live in abundance. I have learned in any and all circumstances the secret of facing every situation, whether well-fed or going hungry, having a sufficiency and enough to spare or going without and being in want. I have strength for all things in Christ Who empowers me [I am ready for anything and equal to anything through Him Who infuses inner strength into me; I am self-sufficient in Christ's sufficiency]" (Amplified).

Conclusion

As I close this chapter, I invite you to take a moment to review and apply this biblical profile to your own life and leadership. What are your areas of strength and what areas are in need of significant improvement? What steps might you take this week to become the kind of effective Christian leader we have discussed? Perhaps you may want to extend this and set yourself priority targets for the next month, quarter, or year. Remember, the key is becoming more like Jesus. Character transformation is truly possible only as He molds us.

QUESTIONS FOR DISCUSSION

1. What aspects of the Christian leader's profile seem most challenging to you?

2. Do you think that we should always consider this biblical profile when selecting Christian leaders? Are there other equally important considerations?

3. What changes in our procedures or structure do we need to make to improve our election/selection process?

Christian Leadership—
An Honorable Ambition

"To aspire to leadership is an honourable ambition" (1 Tim. 3:1, NEB).
"Should you then seek great things for yourself? Seek them not"
(Jer. 45:5, NIV).

As we have alluded to, normally the church does not look favorably on those who openly demonstrate a desire for leadership. Many assume that the person who does not want the office is the one that should receive the responsibility. Such an attitude conjures the image of a reluctant conscript being labored with to accept a position for which he or she claims to have no longing. Our typical approach has been that it is better for the position to seek out the person than for the person to seek out the position.

Of course, it may be that the potential office seeker's reluctance merely masks a deep inner interest that the aspirant dares not reveal for fear of ostracism given our traditional outlook. I once spoke with a colleague about an administrative position for which many felt he was eminently qualified. He responded with a passionate denial of any interest in that position, only to accept it within a few minutes after the nominating committee contacted him.

Someone uncomfortable with the perspective that it is not wrong to desire an office will introduce God's call of biblical individuals such as Moses. After all, he was as reluctant as they come. I acknowledge this, for it is possible for a summons to a particular ministry to come as a shock, and thus initially meet a genuine negative response. While some people have the desire before the call, others receive the call to serve before the desire has awakened. However, whether the call has been an ongoing passion or has been stimulated by divine revelation, human persuasion, or a dawning personal conviction, desire is still necessary for effectiveness. The fire may be slow to ignite, but it will come. Once you get hot, others will feel the flame! Your passion and its effects will be seen. This was the case with

Moses as passion replaced his initial hesitation. (By the way, Moses had another reason for his reluctance to accept the divine summons to return to Egypt. Its authorities wanted him for murder!)

It is true that untamed ambition can cause personal and corporate ruin and has led to the downfall of many great leaders in society and even in the church. An unholy desire to control, to decide the fate of others, spells grave danger for any organization, and the church must be wary of those who seek office merely for the office's sake.

Surely we need to avoid such unholy ambition. In the second text quoted above, Jeremiah counseled his scribe Baruch not to seek great things for himself. The context clearly suggests, however, that it was not a condemnation of all ambition, but rather an indictment of selfish motivation that makes all consequent ambition wrong. It is the "seeking of great things for *yourself*" that is wrong and sinful and that has no place in the church or any Christian organization.

But Paul tells us that aspiring to leadership is an honorable ambition. Desiring to be a Christian leader is not automatically sinful. It is your motivation that determines the character of your ambition. Do you wish to hold office to draw attention to yourself and to soak up the power, privilege, and prestige associated with today's corporate and national leaders? Or do you have a flaming passion to make a difference for God's kingdom, and to be single-minded for your salvation and that of others? Paul epitomized this latter spirit when he wrote: "I consider them [everything else] rubbish, that I may gain Christ" (Phil. 3:8, NIV). Holy desire and ambition has its rightful place.

I see this holy desire and passion in Joshua conquering the land, in David's onslaughts against the enemies of Israel, in Nehemiah's restoring of the wall, in Paul's never-quit attitude in spite of unrelenting persecution. Holy ambition is a desire to do all for Christ, to elevate Him, to deny self, and to enjoy the freedom and fulfillment of doing God's will. It is a willingness even to suffer personally in order to further God's purposes. Only you know what truly fuels your passion. And what drives your desire to lead is essential in determining whether or not such ambition is holy or unholy.

It is interesting to review the context in which Paul wrote that aspiring to leadership is an honorable ambition. The environment for leaders was quite different from what it is today. In his day Christian leaders endured constant hardship, contempt, rejection, and personal sacrifice for the cause of God. The leader was the first to suffer persecution and often stood at the forefront of the dangers facing the church. Seen in this context, the apostle's counsel becomes more understandable. He was saying that in spite of the difficulties and sacrifices associated with Christian leadership, it is still honorable to aspire to that role, to advance the mission of Christ. In answer to those who may have been afraid to preach, you can imagine Paul's response being "Woe is unto me if I preach not" (1 Cor. 9:16).

Thus Paul's statement in 1 Timothy 3 is not an endorsement for the unworthy and the self-seeking. Nor is it an offer of privileged working conditions and enviable retirement benefits. Church leadership is not an opportunity to lord it over other believers. Above all, it is not a guarantee of infallibility. Paul's statement simply acknowledges that, in spite of the dangers, loss, and woe, a deep love for Christ and the advance of His cause still provide a good motivation for desiring church leadership.

James Berkley observes that "no minister wants to be perceived as self-centeredly ambitious. Yet what church would want a complacent pastor with no discernible ambition? . . . Good, holy ambition drives the mills of excellent ministry, helps us accomplish tasks the unambitious might deem impossible, transforms churches, and maximizes gifts. . . . Why should the church with the most important assignment in the world offer responsibilities to people who have no desire for them? We certainly won't adopt that approach when managing our earthly affairs. Then why do it when managing kingdom business?" (*Leadership Handbooks of Practical Theology, Volume 3: Leadership and Administration; Ambition and Contentment*, pp. 23, 24).

Because of its root meaning, the word "ambition"—even when modified by the adjective "holy"—may cause concern when used in the context of Christian leadership. The word comes from a Latin word meaning "campaigning for promotion." Some congregations and denominations regard campaigning for promotion as unacceptable. However, others encourage it. While I served at the Interdenominational Theological Center in Atlanta in 1999, I attended a rally by W. Franklyn Richardson, who was seeking the leadership of the National Baptist Convention, USA, Inc. He supplied the audience with a 12-point vision for the organization that he hoped to implement if elected president. Richardson lost in that election, and again in 2004, to William J. Shaw, of Philadelphia, Pennsylvania.

To some other faith communities, the campaigning approach is taboo. Yet it may take place in their ranks in more subtle and perhaps devious ways. If you have been close to church leadership, you are probably aware of some of the undesirable methods that persons eager to secure leadership roles have employed. Pressure groups develop around election times, and they attempt to do the work of the Holy Spirit in determining who should and should not hold office. Let me underscore that whatever methods employed to arrive at the selection or election of Christian leaders, the key elements present ought to be honesty, transparency, and a desire to let God lead in the process. To revert to unchristian practices in the pursuit of a Christian leadership role clearly reveals the nature of that motivation.

If the motivation is right, we should have no objection to people indicating their willingness to serve in certain areas. As a church pastor I used service interest inventories to guide the nominating committee to people it might ask to hold the various offices. The system served us well at the local level. Perhaps we should consider something similar at other levels of denominational service. The goal is to offer opportunities to people who want to serve.

Perhaps we should try a system like that employed by the National Baptist Convention, one that allows people who wish to lead the organization to state what visions they have for the future of the organization, and then letting the people—all of them—decide. The unofficial results in the 2004 election indicate that Shaw defeated Richardson, taking 68 percent of the vote (9,458 to 13,934) (see www.nationalbaptist.com).

It would be refreshing in the Seventh-day Adventist Church to have two or three finalists share with the church their visions for the future of the organization and how they would lead it into that future. What are their ideas for evangelistic growth, for the educational and health programs, for the publishing and mass communication ministries, for youth and families, for structural reorganization to function effectively in the twenty-first century? What's the vision that God has placed on their hearts for carrying forward His global mission? Let's hear it, let's pray about it, and then, as the Spirit leads, let's cast lots. That would be a new day for transparency and inclusiveness in the church!

A well-ordered public election process would reduce the back-room deals and promises that cloud some current models. Whether we label it election, selection, or nomination, choosing leaders is a political process, and the challenge is to make that process Christlike. People in the biblical model prayed and cast lots. The church has to strive today to ensure that all processes are open, transparent, and Spirit-directed. It may mean a longer and more thorough work for nominating committees. Indeed, their roles may change to being more of a search committee that makes recommendations to the delegates at a session. But these changes are well worth considering.

But let's get back to the issue of ambition. Jesus has given us the kind of ambition that should undergird Christian leadership, one diametrically opposed to the secular concept.

"But Jesus called them to Himself and said to them, 'You know that those who are considered rulers over the Gentiles lord it over them, and their great ones exercise authority over them. Yet it shall not be so among you; but whoever desires to become great among you shall be your servant. And whoever of you desires to be first shall be slave of all'" (Mark 10:42-44, NKJV).

Christian leadership is servant leadership. It is found in losing oneself in service to others, not in coaxing or inducing others to serve you and your interests. In a word, it is *servanthood*. Most people associate servanthood with lowliness in value, respect, and honor, but Jesus revolutionized the concept by using it as a synonym for greatness.

Jesus had two disciples who shared an unholy ambition for greatness. They used their conniving mother to approach Him to request top positions for them in the coming kingdom. James and John fancied the idea of sitting on glorious thrones and judging Israel. But Jesus' response was "Ye know not what ye ask" (verse 38). Their plotting aroused the hostility of the other 10 and led Jesus to expound two essential principles for Christian leadership. I am indebted to J. Oswald Saunders (*Spiritual Leadership*) for his clear insights on those principles.

1. The Divine Sovereignty of Christian Leadership. Jesus reminded His disciples that "to sit at my right or left is not for me to grant. These places belong to those for whom they have been prepared" (verse 40, NIV).

It is God who assigns places of spiritual ministry and leadership. While it may appear that a popular election or a committee has selected a leader, it is God at work using human measures to extend His sacred call to service. Thus if God is for it, it will stand. But if it is not His sovereign will, all our human machinations will eventually amount to zero. In His overarching will, God sometimes allows wrong choices to play their course (just as He permitted Israel to spend 40 years on a journey that should have taken 40 days), but in the end His purposes always prevail.

Gideon was another leader of great faith and implicit confidence in a mighty God. His victorious leadership of 300 men in conquest against 135,000 took place only through complete dependence on God. He recognized that his success came not by his own might or power, but by the Spirit of God. Thus when in the thrill of success the people sought to appoint him king, he faithfully affirmed that neither he nor his son would govern them, but "the Lord will rule over you" (Judges 8:23, NIV). Clearly Gideon affirmed that God is in ultimate control in human affairs, and that He uses whomever He chooses to accomplish His purpose.

This principle of divine appointment should provide much assurance to Christian leaders. We can then safely say that we are where we are because of God's will and can therefore fulfill the responsibilities of our office without fear or favor, for it is He who sets up and it is He who takes down. Actually, I do not like the concept of up or down. Rather, it is God working with us through all of life's situations, for He never leaves us or forsakes us. He continues to direct our paths whether we are in or out of office.

Having the conviction that God has called you to lead gives you confidence to deal with the myriad challenges that you face in leadership. On my first visit to a new congregation a senior elder pulled me aside and informed me that he usually gave pastors trouble. I surveyed him for a moment. Clearly he seemed to be a veteran of many church wars! But I simply responded with a wry smile that I love elders who give me trouble.

He repeated his assertion, for he felt I hadn't taken him seriously. To which I repeated, "That's OK! I love elders who give me trouble."

"Pastor, you don't understand!" he persisted. "I give pastors real trouble!"

"I really love elders who give me real trouble," I again emphasized.

Initially he was indeed a difficult member to deal with, but through prayer and care under the leadership of the Spirit of God, I developed a wonderful relationship with him and his family. It included several lunch dates at their home and home-baked cakes on special occasions that his wife baked and he cheerfully delivered. Leaders need to have a confidence born out of the conviction that God has placed them in a particular position for that time.

2. The Suffering of Christian Leadership. Jesus asked the two aspiring disciples, "Can you drink the cup I drink and be baptized with the baptism I am baptized with?" (Mark 10:38, NIV). Here Jesus sets forth the cost of serving in His kingdom. He reminds His disciples then—and us today—that the cost of discipleship is suffering, deprivation, and (for most of the early disciples) painful death. A call to Christian leadership is a summons to tread the winepress with our Lord. Suffering and servanthood are inexorably linked in the life of the Christian leader.

After supper in the upper room, Jesus proceeded to wash His disciples' feet. Rising from His task, He reaffirmed His lordship and indicated that lordship is about service. Peter also reminds us that Jesus left an example of suffering for us to follow (1 Peter 2:21). The life and teaching of our Lord yoked service and suffering together, and so they will be in the lives of His people today.

In my years in pastoral ministry I have heard such expressions from colleagues as "If you can't master, you can't pastor." Another was "Preachers don't swing mops—only deacons do." I have also seen some leaders show obvious displeasure at what they interpreted as a lack of expected courtesies. Like secular leaders, some Christian leaders today demand more pomp and ceremony to surround them, and their trappings seem more consistent with an earthly king than the meek and lowly Galilean! That is not to say that Christian leaders should live a pitiable existence, but it is worrying that many church leaders today crave isolation and insulation from any discomfort. Jesus warned, "Beware of the scribes, who desire to go around in long robes, love greetings in the marketplaces, the best seats in the synagogues, and the best places at feasts" (Mark 12:38, 39, NKJV).

William Johnsson, retired editor of the *Adventist Review,* explains that during the time of Jesus the Sadducees handled the Temple services, and they gained great wealth from this role. Pilgrims who came to worship had to change their money into the Temple coinage and then purchase animals supplied by the Temple. The Temple authorities benefited handsomely from both types of transaction. What should have been a house of prayer for all nations had deteriorated into a moneymaking scheme that exploited the common people and made the religious leaders rich (*Adult Teachers Sabbath School Bible Study Guide*, April-June 2005, p. 96). No wonder Jesus had to chase the money changers out of the Temple (Mark 11:15-17)!

Do we see a similar trend today in the merchandising of the gospel with the emphasis on the sale of books, study guides, tapes, videos, CDs, and DVDs? Isn't it a cause for concern when preaching and singing evangelists seem to be more interested in the sale of tapes than in the salvation of souls? Shouldn't we worry when the quality of the nearby golf courses and shopping malls determine the locations of our conferences and retreats more than the prudent stewardship of limited financial resources? Are we not to question the motives of Christian leaders who appear to be taking more from and giving less to their organizations? While such a spirit is by no means pervasive, yet we do find evidence to indicate that some Christian leaders have gone a long way from the model of the Suffering Servant!

Furthermore, Christian leaders whose ambition is driven by zeal for the glory of God will not be strident or flamboyant, will not engage in ego trips and arrogant self-advertising, but rather will seek to be humble and self-effacing, ever striving to model the simplicity and grace of Christ. They will be sympathetic with the weak, merciful with the erring, gentle with the hard-hearted, gracious to those who hold different opinions, and kind even to those who wish them pain and suffering. It is as we model such qualities that we truly follow our Suffering Servant who, without concern for personal well-being, pursued His life calling, which was simply to go about "doing good."

The Ultimate Success of Christian Leadership

To the two principles highlighted by Sanders, I would add a third one. As Christian leaders, we can remain joyous whatever the prevailing circumstances, for we know that we are on the winning team. Like the child who has already read the happy ending to the book, we can smile in the midst of the dark days, for we know how the story ends.

Even in the here and now, it is hard to ignore the deep joys and successes we enjoy as Christian leaders. Except for Judas, the lives of the disciples demonstrated unswerving zeal and love until their death. Their ministry was satisfying and fulfilling, and they obviously wanted to do nothing else. When we review our ministry and recount the numerous lives transformed, bodies healed, homes reestablished, careers redirected, marriages saved, church congregations established, leaders trained, and students that have excelled in various fields of endeavor—we can all say to ourselves that it has been worth it.

Thank-you notes, baptismal ceremonies, anniversaries, graduation events, marriages, and mortgage-burning occasions are all times we find it difficult to withhold the tears of joy. Above all, the silent Spirit-inspired acknowledgment within our own souls that we have done the best for our Master and Lord truly defines our success in Christian leadership. Henry and Richard Blackaby note that "those spiritual leaders who refuse to compromise their Christianity while leading their organization will know tremendous satisfaction at the end of their journey, and they will be able to sleep at night along the way" (*Spiritual Leadership*, p. 272).

Questions for Discussion

1. Does ambition have a place in Christian leadership?

2. What would make a desire to serve in a specific role healthy or unhealthy?

3. What practices and trends among Christian leaders and organizations especially concern you? Why? Is it possible that some activities may raise questions in the minds of some onlookers but not others? What should be the response of the leader in such situations? What should be the response of onlookers?

7 The Essence of Effectiveness

We have already talked about the urgent need for leaders to serve the rapidly growing needs of the Seventh-day Adventist Church. Both paid employees and volunteer personnel are absolutely essential to the accomplishment of our global mission. From our understanding of Christian stewardship, we believe that the Holy Spirit has gifted every member for roles in building up the body of Christ, and Paul reminds us that "it is required in stewards, that a man be found faithful" (1 Cor. 4:2). Thus our goal is to find leaders who can be truly effective in their work. Our stewardship commitment is a summons to effectiveness in every aspect of our lives. In whatever area of leadership we are in, doing our best for the long-term impact must be our watchword.

But what are the defining elements of effective leadership? Many ideas surface from different authors and leadership theorists, but three seem to keep coming up again and again. They are (1) vision, (2) passion, and (3) action. Let's take a closer look at them.

Vision

The first responsibility of a leader is to forge a shared vision of a desired future reality. When asked, "What could be worse than being born without sight?" Helen Keller replied, "Being born with sight and no vision."

A vision is a mental description of a desired future reality. Vision is seeing with the mind's eye what is possible in people, in projects, in causes, and in enterprises. Such vision results when our mind joins need with possibility. William Blake said, "What is now proved was once only imagined." For the Christian leader a vision is not a destination or a location but a journey. It is sensing where God is directing and then following His path.

Former General Conference of Seventh-day Adventists president Robert H. Pierson was right on target in describing a leader with vision:

"A leader with vision sees souls in now dark counties and countries. He sees church buildings where now there are only vacant lots. To the worker with vision there are no Alps, no Rockies, no Everests! His valiant, unfettered faith surmounts all obstacles. Evangelistic efforts, schools, hospitals, clinics, church buildings, spring up under the magic of the Master's touch when the man of faith and vision accepts the promises and challenges the omnipotent God" (*So You Want to Be a Leader!* p. 10).

The King James Version translates Proverbs 29:18 as "Where there is no vision, the people perish." Some have understood this to mean that without vision, the people leave for another parish! However, the New International Version gives a clearer understanding of the text: "Where there is no revelation, the people cast off restraint." But I particularly like the *Message* paraphrase: "If people can't see what God is doing, they stumble all over themselves." It concludes: "But when they attend to what he reveals, they are most blessed."

For the Christian leader, vision begins with divine revelation. Through study, prayer, and reflection God's Spirit speaks to us, giving us insights as to how we may order our lives, our homes, and our organizations to fulfill His divine purpose. As Ellen White said of Jesus, committed Christian leaders make no plans for themselves but daily seek to live the unfolding of God's plan for them. Note the full statement:

"Where many have erred was in not being careful in following God's ideas, but their own. Christ Himself declared, 'The Son can do nothing of himself, but what he seeth the Father do' (John 5:19). So utterly was He emptied of Himself that He made no schemes and plans. He lived accepting God's plans for Him, and the Father day by day unfolded His plans. If Jesus was so wholly dependent, and declared, 'Whatsoever I see the Father do, that I do,' how much more should human agents depend upon God for constant instruction, so that their lives might be the simple working out of God's plans!" (*In Heavenly Places*, p. 147).

Having a sense of where God is guiding us, leaders then seek to enroll others in that vision. They understand that leadership is a shared process and seek to build a consensus around the common goal. Such vision will be consistent with the aspirations of the followers. Leaders restate the vision again and again, so that people grasp what the desired future is. The vision needs to be broad and bold. Perhaps that's what Habakkuk meant when he talked about writing the vision so large that even a man running a race would be able to read it (Hab. 2:2).

One cannot overstress the importance of communicating the vision. It must be lit in the pulpit and ignited in the pew. Or it must fire up the boardroom or the classroom. Whatever your assignment may be in your home, church, conference, college, or institution—no matter what your calling may be—your number one responsibility of leadership is to continually clarify and communicate the goal and intent of that particular ministry or service. You must constantly answer the following questions for your people: Why are we here? Why are we doing what we are doing? If you don't know the answers to such questions, you can't lead.

The emerging body of information on emotional intelligence helps us understand how leaders are able to connect and communicate with their followers. EQ is the capacity to be aware of and to regulate your own emotions, and to understand and effectively relate to the emotions of others. Daniel Goleman, one of its leading proponents, describes EQ as "the overlooked yet essential ingredient of leadership" (in *U.S. News and World Report,* Jan. 14, 2002). He has studied leaders from hundreds of companies and found that the higher up the ladder they climbed, the more important their emotional intelligence was to their performance.

Former New York mayor Rudy Giuliani's effectiveness soared after September 11, 2001, when the city and the nation saw a newfound compassion and connectedness to balance his better-known command-and-control style. His empathy brought comfort to millions. Of course, students of Scripture learned about this a long time ago when they read that "for we have not an high priest which cannot be touched with the feeling of our infirmities; but was in all points tempted like as we are, yet without sin" (Heb. 4:15). What the biblical author emphasizes here is what Christians have seen modeled in their Exemplar, Jesus Christ—the ability to lead not only from the head but also from the heart.

Visionary leaders are able to tie their concepts to the felt needs of individual followers so that in accomplishing the corporate vision, all members also meet their own needs. People generally assume that their own goals are good ones, while the goals of others are not necessarily in their best interests. Therefore, the effective leader always seeks to understand the needs of his followers and to integrate them into the corporate vision. A good example of this is a church that raises thousands of dollars for its feed-the-hungry program by hosting an annual dinner. Hundreds of people pay $50 to dress up in fine formal wear, go to a prestigious hotel, and dine on a bread roll and a bowl of soup! They are happy to do so, knowing that they are contributing to a worthy cause.

Effective leaders can cast an exciting vision but can also balance that vision with reality. Not into sentimentalities, they are quite prepared to call a spade a spade, rather than an elongated horticultural instrument. Their plain, forthright interpretation of reality helps to calm nerves and alleviate fears. Such ability to remain positive and to keep encouraging and motivating followers, in spite of reverses and missteps, are key elements in their effectiveness.

Regrettably, too many leaders in church offices lack any sense of what they might achieve. They just stand in the way and passively wait to react to whatever may come from the pastor, the board, or the conference office. But leaders differ from managers because they are creative and willing to act on their own initiative. Jere Patzer, president of the North Pacific Union Conference of the Seventh-day Adventist Church, argues that "if our church were ever to die, it wouldn't be because of attacks from the self-righteousness of the radical right or from the Laodicea of the liberal left. It would be because those of us leaders in the middle of the road have lost our vision" (*The Road Ahead*, p. 47).

Several years ago I served as pastor at the Willesden Seventh-day Adventist Church in west London, England. When I first arrived, the division, union, and conference officials determined which churches they wanted to preach at and simply assigned themselves on the preaching schedules. Local pastors awaited the arrival of these schedules to see where vacant spaces remained for them to schedule themselves or other speakers.

I objected to that practice, for it precluded long-range planning at the local level and resulted in a disjointed ministry. Sometimes the local pastor had to plan around six visiting speakers for the quarter, all coming with their differing emphases. As the leader of the local congregation, I felt that the local leaders and I were better placed to determine which speakers and which emphases we wanted at any given time.

On one occasion, therefore, I informed one of the officials that our church could not accommodate him on the date he had indicated. He let me know that he considered my position shocking and revolutionary and that he would speak to my conference president on the matter. But I remained calm and unequivocal in my stand. We did welcome him to our church at a later date, when the local leadership felt that his ministry fitted in with the specific emphasis of the congregation at that time.

Passion

Passion comes from the heart and manifests itself in optimism, excitement, and emotional connection. It fires unrelenting drive. Stephen Covey calls it your voice (*The Eighth Habit*, p. 5)—what energizes your life and gives you drive, keeping you at it when everything else says quit. Individuals whose passion intersects with their jobs do not require any supervision. They manage themselves and go the extra mile because of the fire that burns from within.

E. Glenn Wagner, founder and president of FutureLead, recalls listening as E. V. Hill shared what is clearly the heart and soul of passionate leadership. Asked to speak on the Great Commission found in Matthew 28:19, 20, Hill told of a time that the Black Panthers were active in the United States. As they roamed the streets of New York, stores in some parts of the city began closing at 5:00 p.m. Report after report confirmed that their presence and activity had begun spreading a sense of fear.

So Hill asked his audience, "How many Black Panthers were actually active in New York City? How many of them did it take to cause store owners to lock up their establishments or churches not to have worship at night? How many of them kept Central Park deserted at night and filled the town with fear? What was the active membership of the Black Panther Party of New York City?"

His answer created a stunned silence. "Eighty-one." Hill then drove home his point.

"Eighty-one running 4 million people across the bridges. Eighty-one closing down churches and businesses. Eighty-one causing fear and shutting down the places of social activity. Just 81!" He paused briefly and then continued, "My friends, we should condemn the Black Panthers' activities, but we also should compliment them for their effectiveness! Those 81 people were dedicated to their cause to the point of risking their own lives, not caring what could possibly happen to them. As a result, they nearly closed down New York City" (Rick Warren, *Ministry Toolbox*, Aug. 3, 2005).

The apostle Paul is a prime biblical example of that kind of passion. In Acts 20 we learn of his planned trip to Jerusalem, where bonds and afflictions awaited him and he would likely face death. But he was determined to go. His attitude was: "I am ready not to be bound only, but also to die at Jerusalem for the name of the Lord Jesus" (Acts 21:13). He was prepared to do whatever the Spirit called him to do at whatever cost, for however long. If he lost his life in the process, so be it.

While we rejoice at the growth of the Seventh-day Adventist Church in numerous parts of the world, North America and Western Europe remain a matter of concern. In *A Guide to Marketing Adventism* Dan Day states that North American Adventism today typically appeals to those with a more pragmatic, nonemotional perspective on life.

"Adventist church services tend to be rather sedate experiences. We sing well but not with particular enthusiasm. Our prayers are complex and well-considered, rather than inspired. Our sermons are well thought out and biblically sound, rather than charged with power and conviction. People leave reassured, rather than revived" (p. 140).

Compare this image with the passion, fervor, and enthusiasm that electrified the early church and still appears in growing congregations today.

G. Ralph Thompson, former executive secretary of the General Conference, observed that all organizations go through three phases in their life cycle. First is the pioneering or missionary stage. It is a time of passion, fervor, and enthusiastic sacrificial endeavors. The second phase involves the creation of institutions. Here the organization concerns itself with the establishment of schools, hospitals, conferences, and so forth. The Seventh-day Adventist Church as a unit has been in this phase for some time. The third phase in the life cycle is one of fossilizing—a period of decline, decay, and ultimate death of the organization. Evangelize, institutionalize, or fossilize. Which phase is your local organization in?

When communicating their passion for an initiative, leaders need to be sensitive to their environment. In a Christian organization the leader's passion must not ride roughshod over the collective wisdom of the body. At the 2005 General Conference session of the Seventh-day Adventist Church president Jan Paulsen emphasized the need for consultation and consensus in decision-making. Leaders will demonstrate vision and passion, but in so doing, they need to work with the organization, not apart from it. Loose cannons are a danger both to personal and organizational safety.

Young enthusiastic leaders need to exercise great sensitivity in offering suggestions or recommending changes to the church hierarchy, because older leaders sometimes regard them with suspicion. There has to be balance, for not every new idea is a bad idea, nor is every old one a good one. While seniority does not confer infallible wisdom, youth need to recognize that what they want to build on currently is there only because of the efforts of those who went before them. The effective leader therefore combines passion with wisdom.

Action

It's hard to get people excited merely on a vision. They like to see something happening. No one wants to get into a vehicle that's going nowhere! Wherever and whenever possible, it's a good idea to celebrate mini-victories along the way to big achievements. This maintains the momentum for further progress.

Several years ago the local conference asked me to lead a congregation that had been in a church building program for almost 10 years. The vision was there, but the prolonged lack of activity had led to low morale, disenchantment, and declining attendance, as members voted with their feet. The atmosphere in the church was quite depressing. In fact, people had dubbed the unsightly, unfinished structure in which they worshipped the "cattle shed." Determined not to be a "cattle shed" pastor, I had to do something quick.

With the support of the local conference administration, we secured a loan to provide a financial lease of life to the project. We also mobilized the members to support the building program. In faith, we set a date nine months away for the dedication of the new facilities. With builders on site and heavy equipment rolling, excitement began to build. Hope sprang alive, and contributions to the project increased significantly. Slogans and buzzwords captured the spirit. The momentum became electrifying, with messages such as "Let the west be the best"; "Work day and night, for dedication is in sight." By the grace of God we completed the facility and formally opened it on schedule with only a small remaining debt.

With the new facilities, the membership quickly grew, and so did the church finances. As a result, we were able to eliminate the indebtedness easier and earlier than we would have if we had waited to raise the funds prior to proceeding with construction. People will be excited and give to a planned project for a time, but if they do not see any movement toward realizing their dream, they will walk away—emotionally, financially, and even physically.

Leadership requires a pioneering spirit. Whether directing a personal ministries council, the conference Adventist Youth department, or an Adventist college, leaders who make a difference are those not afraid to try unorthodox methods or stretch the boundaries. They have a bias for action, and they do things with a sense of urgency. Wanting to see something done yesterday, for today is too late, they cut through bureaucratic red tape to get to the finish line. Such leaders recognize that in a competitive environment, slow and cumbersome organizations will wind up second every time.

In the local church setting, for instance, the goal is the spiritual and numerical growth of the congregation. Holding series of meetings and conducting various programs and conferences are good, but at the end of the day the important questions are: Are people growing in Jesus? Are they being saved? Similarly, the goal for teachers is students who have learned; for doctors, patients who have been restored to health; and for a family, happiness, wholeness, and general well-being. What's the finish line for your leadership endeavor? Do you have a clear line of sight to it?

We often give the impression that success as a leader automatically results in increased responsibilities, somewhat like a ladder of roles and responsibilities. Some have believed that you should be a deacon before you get "promoted" to the eldership. If a pastor is successful, he gets "advanced" to the conference office. A good academic program or department chair gets elevated to deanship or vice president. Many measure success by whether one gets "called" up the church echelons. Within the Seventh-day Adventist Church structure, such promotions would be to the local conference, union, division, or General Conference.

But for the truly effective leader, a successful career is a growing reputation for making things happen for the glory of God while nurturing effective relationships. If you are able to make flowers bloom in whatever desert you are in—if the long-term impact of your leadership creates people who sense that they have been blessed and benefited and had their lives transformed—then you are an effective leader, regardless of whether your life service is global or merely local.

A leader's level of credibility will also influence the ability to motivate others to action. Credibility is a fund of goodwill that the leader has acquired. It is like a deposit in a bank account. The leader adds to or subtracts from this fund of good will, based on the effectiveness of his or her performance. Those with high credibility are able to accomplish much more and take more risks with the support of their followers. A leader who lacks such recognition may be raring to go, but no one is willing to follow. When that happens, the leader must either seek to rebuild that credit or acknowledge the need for a new assignment.

Bill Hybels, senior pastor of the Willow Creek Church in Chicago, talks about the reverse situation, when the followers are ready to move but the leader stalls. Hybels admits that he sometimes gets frustrated at "the meandering pace of Kingdom advancement," because those of us who lead it don't want to lose very much in the advancement process (*20/20 Vision–Leadership Principles From Acts 20*, p. 10). He observes that if advancement might cost us our reputation, criticism, money, or people's pleasure, we back down. Some maintenance leaders are prepared to do only the minimum to sustain the organization, and thus they avoid taking any risks or exercising any initiatives.

Calvin Rock, former world vice president for the Seventh-day Adventist Church, declared that "such leaders have decided that the best way to make it to the top or to survive to the end is to drift with the tide. They are more concerned with institutional benefits than with institutional viability. Their motto is 'Play it safe, and if you're lucky you'll get moved or promoted before the roof caves in.' Being more concerned with not getting into trouble than with the triumph of the cause, they struggle to survive and advance, and while they often advance as individuals, the cause of God does not" (*Church Leadership—A Call to Virtue*, p. 75).

But effective Christian leadership is not about survival or mere maintenance—it's not even about being well liked or popular. Rather, it's about fulfilling your divine call and obedience to God. I like George Barna's reinterpretation of the parable of the rich young ruler in Mark 10:17-23. Focusing on the primacy of obedience in Christian leadership, Barna frames the story this way:

"As Jesus started on his way, a man came up to him and fell on his knees. 'Good teacher,' he asked, 'what must I do to be a great leader who is Christian?'

"'Why do you call me good?' Jesus answered. 'No one is good except God alone. You know the requirements: cast God's vision, motivate people to pursue it, mobilize them efficiently, strategically guide their efforts, and develop the resources necessary to fulfill the vision.'

"'Teacher,' he declared, 'all these things I have done since I have been a leader.'

"Jesus looked at him and loved him. 'One thing you lack,' he said. 'Change your philosophy of leadership from achieving success to being obedient, and you will truly be useful to your Father in heaven.'

"At this the man's face fell. He went away because he had great success in leadership.

"Jesus looked around and said to his disciples, 'How hard it is for the leaders of this world to lead in ways that honor God'" (*A Fish Out of Water*, p. 189).

My leader friend, in the midst of our vision, passion, and action, please seek to be a leader who honors God.

QUESTIONS FOR DISCUSSION

1. What should Christian leaders do if their members or followers do not share their vision?

2. Is it easier for some personalities to show passion? Or can one demonstrate passion in different ways?

3. What strategies could a Christian leader adopt to stay energized? What role does divine connection play?

8

A Call to Excellence

In youthful exuberance I sat glued to my portable black-and-white television set as Muhammad Ali knocked out his opponent and captured the world heavyweight boxing title for the third time. In utter ecstasy and triumphant jubilation he screamed to the excited reporters and cameramen, "I am the greatest! I am the greatest! I am the greatest!" Millions of Ali fans around the world, including me, echoed the victorious chant, "Ali is the greatest!"

Such a display of self-aggrandizement is obviously unthinkable for the Christian. On the other hand, is it possible for Christian leaders to achieve excellence while glorifying their Maker rather than themselves? Let's explore this question by considering the life of an ancient leader who exhibited the same self-glorifying tendencies as Muhammad Ali.

The ancient city of Babylon, where the modern city of Baghdad now stands, long served as the capital of Mesopotamia. Although a mere 10 miles in circumference, the site had become an international center of commerce, trade, and industry. Its inhabitants referred to the city as "the origin and center of all lands."

Werner Keller says of Babylon: "Its ancient power and glory had no equal in the ancient world" (*The Bible as History*, p. 289). Isaiah referred to the city as "the jewel of kingdoms, the glory of the Babylonians' pride" (Isa. 13:19, NIV). Here was Babylon, the great ancient city, and its builder and king was Nebuchadnezzar.

From all accounts, his administrative style echoed that of many leaders today. A raging conqueror, a proud autocrat, and a compulsive builder, he comes across as having an unrelenting hunger for greatness. In Daniel 4:30 we see him beating his chest and exclaiming, "Is not this great Babylon, that I have built for the house of the kingdom by the might of my power, and for the honor of my majesty?"

Some may wonder why we should even discuss such a selfish despot in a book on Christian leadership. What does he have to teach us? But I plead for a moment of tolerance even for this strong-willed leader. Maybe we should not write him off completely, for I see in him a quality worth reflecting upon.

Nebuchadnezzar never settled for less than the best. His flaming desire to be the first ever, the best ever, and the biggest ever certainly sprang from the wrong motivation, for he seemed to be on a continuous ego trip. Like Hitler in more recent times, Nebuchadnezzar was zealous only in promoting himself so as to receive worldly praise and attention. A committed Christian, on the other hand, should be motivated by a love for God and a desire to glorify His name. Nebuchadnezzar's motivation, like that of Muhammad Ali, is not acceptable for the Christian, and we should reject it outright.

But what about striving for excellence? Could there be something positive about this trait? I believe so. Note the following passages of Scripture:

"Be ye therefore perfect, even as your Father which is in heaven is perfect" (Matt. 5:48).

"Therefore leaving the principles of the doctrine of Christ, let us go on unto perfection" (Heb. 6:1).

Add to these the following statements from Ellen White:

"Be content with nothing less than perfection" (*Messages to Young People*, p. 73).

"The Lord requires perfection from His redeemed family. He expects from us the perfection which Christ reached in his humanity" (*Child Guidance*, p. 477).

"Glorious is the hope before the believer as he advances by faith toward the height of Christian perfection!" (*The Acts of the Apostles*, p. 533).

By perfection she means excellence at every stage of life and in every area of activity. And the great news is that we are not left to fight alone against our natural inclinations to mediocrity. No, we are assured of success as we allow the Lord to take full control of our lives, for it is "God who works in [me] to will and to act according to his good purpose" (Phil. 2:13, NIV).

Thus the desire for excellence should motivate every Christian. We should be determined to be our best and do our best, not for the sake of earthly plaudits and trinkets or for position or prestige, but to glorify the name of our Maker and Redeemer. To do less is to be negligent in our stewardship obligation as one called to church leadership.

E. G. White wrote: "It is a duty we owe to our Creator to cultivate and improve upon the talents He has committed to our trust" (*Testimonies for the Church,* vol. 3, p. 160). Earlier she rebuked a couple by telling them: "Had you improved the talents lent you of God, you would have shone as lights in the world" (*ibid.*, p. 65).

James 4:17 affirms that "anyone, then, who knows the good he ought to do and doesn't do it, sins" (NIV). Another way of expressing this concept is: "To him that could be extraordinary but contents to be ordinary, to him it is sin." Dedicated Christian leaders will want to be as nearly perfect human instruments as it is possible for them to be, through the grace of God and for the glory of His name.

A crew of masons was engaged in laying bricks near the roof in a huge cathedral. Just before quitting time one of them told the foreman that he had just noticed a row of bricks out of line. "What should I do?" queried the worker as he thought about having to redo the whole row.

After taking a brief look, the foreman said, "Nobody will see this up here, buddy! Work it so!"

Sometime later the same crew was on another project when someone detected a fault in the work already done. "We are not building a cathedral," the leader responded. "Work it so!" It wasn't long before he became known as the "work it so" foreman.

This "work it so" disease also afflicts many Christian leaders. Maintenance becomes the norm as they continue to do just what they did last year. By their continued routine actions, they say, "That's good enough; we'll work it so!" Such church officers may occupy offices, but they hardly allow those offices to occupy their minds and interest. They supply numerous excuses for their inertia and proclaim by their inactivity, "We'll work it so!"

Leaders, how often do we sit on committees and look for the quick solutions rather than the best solutions? We shirk from expending the time and energy to do the best for our Master! Yes, we too are under pressure to join with that mason foreman in declaring, "We'll work it so." But unlike him, we are building spiritual cathedrals for the King of kings.

We are to seek excellence in all we do, for in so doing we glorify God. "Glorify God in your body, and in your spirit," exhorts the apostle Paul (1 Cor. 6:20). "The love of Christ constraineth us," he exclaims again (2 Cor. 5:14). Divine love simply leaves us no choice. Our pursuit of excellence is an inevitable consequence of our stewardship commitment to the Lord. We thus glorify God as we stretch our minds and our bodies to the fullest. That same Creator-God who unravels to humanity the mysteries of space and the marvels of modern computer technology challenges His stewards to rise higher than the highest human thought can reach. Godlikeness is our goal (Ellen G. White, *Education*, p. 18).

Whether as president, pastor, professor, professional, parent, or person in the pew, we should let a commitment to excellence characterize all our endeavors. Personal growth and achievement must always be evident in our lives! Even when failures occur, as surely they will, let the world see that we can grow from them rather than pitifully mourn our misfortunes. If as infants we had failed to rise again after our first falls, we would still be crawling on our knees today.

It needs to be emphasized that our achievements are not solo efforts. In *Patriarchs and Prophets* we read that "the secret of success is the union of divine power with human effort" (p. 509). Thus we see that both God and humanity have separate and distinct roles to perform in an individual's success. We know that the Lord always assures us of the divine power. The critical factor, therefore, is the human effort.

Forever improving should be the Christian's watchword. Even in eternity we will always have "new heights to surmount, new wonders to admire, new truths to comprehend, fresh objects to call forth the powers of mind and soul and body" (*The Great Controversy*, p. 677). Growth and excellence will eternally challenge the Christian.

Nebuchadnezzar's failure lay, not in his divinely ordained desire for excellence, but in his failure to acknowledge God. His focus was on "me, myself, and I." As a leader he had denied the reality of the Ultimate Leader and had usurped the glory due only to God. The same tragedy will befall any who fail to recognize in their achievements the God in whom "we live and move and have our being" (Acts 17:28, NKJV).

But Nebuchadnezzar's experience contains yet another failure. He had set himself up as the source of excellence, when in reality he was merely a reflector of it. Thus he failed to point his followers to the God of his talents and the source of his strength. His failures therefore lay both in his denial of God and in his claiming all the glory for his achievements.

Nebuchadnezzar lost his kingdom until the Babylonian ruler recognized that "the Most High rules in the kingdom of men" (Dan. 4:32, NKJV). No matter how bright the light, it finally goes out when separated from its source of power.

I pray that we will be protected from the failures that ruined this ancient leader. May we ever recognize that all true success involves a partnership between God and humanity. On the other hand, may we always determine to do our best for our Master, knowing that He is always doing His best for us. Let the ringing message of Paul be our life theme: "I can do everything through him who gives me strength" (Phil. 4:13, NIV).

QUESTIONS FOR DISCUSSION

1. Why is the pursuit of excellence a worthy goal for a Christian leader?

2. What should be our attitude toward ongoing mediocrity and lack of adequate preparation in preaching, programs, and overall leadership?

3. How could Christian leaders avoid the temptation to ascribe the successes they achieve to their own unaided efforts?

The Lone Ranger Is Dead

Leadership is not a solo act. To achieve the extraordinary, a leader must have the active involvement and support of others. Some leaders seek to create a competitive spirit among their followers, operating on the principle of "divide and conquer." However, fostering competition among group members is not the route to high performance—fostering teamwork is.

The Church—A Social System

It is important for leaders to recognize the church as a social system. Any system, such as the digestive system in the body or the exhaust system in a car, is characterized by unity of purpose and interdependence of parts. A sense of belonging should bond all in the organization we serve, and we must acknowledge a shared interdependence if the system is to function well.

J. W. Getzels and E. G. Guba have written about organizations as social systems. They refer to two dimensions at work in an organization: the organizational dimension and the individual dimension. The two aspects find themselves in constant tension because of the role expectations of the organization and the needs dispositions of its members. Through a social exchange process (E. P. Hollander, *Leadership Dynamics*) the two dimensions interact and, as a consequence, achieve their goals. In other words, we have needs that the organization fulfills, and the organization has its needs that we fulfill by our participation in it.

Church leaders must realize, therefore, that church structure is not a one-way street. They cannot address a reduction in personal giving, a drop in attendance, or a decline in membership involvement simply by chastisement from the pulpit directed at a lack of spirituality in the pew. A college administrator cannot assume that students will continue to enroll in record numbers, irrespective of college policies. Contented cows give good milk.

Every action produces a reaction. Jesus puts it another way: "Give, and it shall be given unto you" (Luke 6:38).

Delegation Creates New Leaders

In our hierarchical church structure delegation is the primary means of creating more opportunities for leaders. A secure president, pastor, or departmental leader will have no difficulty in sharing responsibility and leadership with his or her colleagues. They will expect their subordinates to work within the boundaries of their responsibilities and authority and to use their gifts in leadership to accomplish the tasks assigned. When delegation does not occur, subordinates find themselves with limited room for creativity. Ideas originate from higher up, where there often exists a bottleneck in decision-making, and the subordinate leaders have to simply "wait for orders." In such a scenario there may be compliance, but little creativity, for all the ideas come from one source.

A conference president once told me that he had ideas for all his departments. He simply wanted hands and feet to implement them. Pat, a social worker and a family friend, tells of the time she went to her boss with some suggestions for improvements. His response was a flat and dismissive "I am not paying you to think. Just do what I tell you." She knew that moment that she had to look for another employer. It is a sad day when we come to believe that we have all the ideas for every area of the organization that we lead. One head with many hands and feet is both a biological and organizational monstrosity! Ellen White reminds us:

"We want every responsible man to drop responsibilities upon others. Set others at work that will require them to plan, and to use judgment. Do not educate them to rely upon your judgment. Young men must be trained up to be thinkers. My brethren, do not for a moment think that your way is perfection, and that those who are connected with you must be your shadows, must echo your words, repeat your ideas, and execute your plans" (*Testimonies to Ministers*, pp. 302, 303).

Delegation helps to unclog the creative and decision-making processes by distributing leadership widely across the organization. But delegation is difficult for some leaders, for they are unwilling to relinquish the jobs that they enjoy. A senior choir leader lamented at a business meeting that she was being cast aside like a used postage stamp. After being director for so long and enjoying it so much, she found it heart-wrenching to surrender the responsibility to an understudy. Several years ago I was asked to serve as a conference director in a certain area, but my predecessor was reluctant to hand over the responsibility. He even kept all the department files and suggested that I come to his office whenever I needed them!

Leaders who believe that they are the only ones who can do the job right will have a major problem with delegation. Once I saw a treasurer rushing around to do everything herself, even though she had four assistants. She refused to share information with her team, believing that it would never be done right if she delegated any of the tasks. She failed to recognize that her assignment was not to do the job, but to manage it. Ellen White explains:

"In some respects the pastor occupies a position similar to that of the foreman of a gang of laboring men or the captain of a ship's crew. They are expected to see that the men over whom they are set do the work assigned to them correctly and promptly, and only in case of emergency are they to execute in detail. The owner of a large mill once found his superintendent in a wheel-pit, making some simple repairs, while a half-dozen workmen in that line were standing by, idly looking on. The proprietor, after learning the facts, so as to be sure that no injustice was done, called the foreman to his office and handed him his discharge with full pay. In surprise the foreman asked for an explanation. It was given in these words: 'I employed you to keep six men at work. I found the six idle, and you doing the work of but one. Your work could have been done just as well by any one of the six. I cannot afford to pay the wages of seven for you to teach the six how to be idle'" (*Christian Service*, p. 70).

She also advised: "The best help that ministers can give the members of our churches is not sermonizing, but planning work for them. Give each one something to do for others. Help all to see that as receivers of the grace of Christ they are under obligation to work for Him. And let all be taught how to work. Especially should those who are newly come to the faith be educated to become laborers together with God" (*Testimonies*, vol. 9, p. 82).

Spiritual Gifts

Teamwork is vital in the Christian community, for the Word of God teaches that no one person can do everything. In 1 Corinthians 12 Paul uses the interconnectedness of the human body to illustrate the point. *The Message* puts it so clearly that it hardly needs elaboration:

"What I want to talk about now is the various ways God's Spirit gets worked into our lives. This is complex and often misunderstood, but I want you to be informed and knowledgeable. . . . God's various gifts are handed out everywhere; but they all originate in God's Spirit. God's various ministries are carried out everywhere; but they all originate in God's Spirit. God's various expressions of power are in action everywhere; but God himself is behind it all. Each person is given something to do that shows who God is: Everyone gets in on it, everyone benefits. All kinds of things are handed out by the Spirit, and to all kinds of people! The variety is wonderful. . . .

"You can easily enough see how this kind of thing works by looking no further than your own body. Your body has many parts—limbs, organs, cells—but no matter how many parts you can name, you're still one body. It's exactly the same with Christ. By means of his one Spirit, we all said good-bye to our partial and piecemeal lives. We each used to independently call our own shots, but then we entered into a large and integrated life in which *he* has the final say in everything. . . . The old labels we once used to identify ourselves—labels like Jew or Greek, slave or free—are no longer useful. We need something larger, more comprehensive.

"I want you to think about how all this makes you more significant, not less. A body isn't just a single part blown up into something huge. It's all the different-but-similar parts arranged and functioning together. If Foot said, 'I'm not elegant like Hand, embellished with rings; I guess I don't belong to this body,' would that make it so? If Ear said, 'I'm not beautiful like Eye, limpid and expressive; I don't deserve a place on the head,' would you want to remove it from the body? If the body was all eye, how could it hear? If all ear, how could it smell? As it is, we see that God has carefully placed each part of the body right where he wanted it.

"But I also want you to think about how this keeps your significance from getting blown up into self-importance. For no matter how significant you are, it is only because of what you are a *part* of. An enormous eye or a gigantic hand wouldn't be a body, but a monster. What we have is one body with many parts, each its proper size and in its proper place. No part is important on its own. Can you imagine Eye telling Hand, 'Get lost; I don't need you'? Or, Head telling Foot, 'You're fired; your job has been phased out'? As a matter of fact, in practice it works the other way—the 'lower' the part, the more basic, and therefore necessary. You can live without an eye, for instance, but not without a stomach. When it's a part of your own body you are concerned with, it makes *no* difference whether the part is visible or clothed, higher or lower. You give it dignity and honor just as it is, without comparisons. If anything, you have more concern for the lower parts than the higher. If you had to choose, wouldn't you prefer good digestion to full-bodied hair?

"The way God designed our bodies is a model for understanding our lives together as a church: every part dependent on every other part, the parts we mention and the parts we don't, the parts we see and the parts we don't. If one part hurts, every other part is involved in the hurt, and in the healing. If one part flourishes, every other part enters into the exuberance" (1 Cor. 12:1-26, Message).

This Pauline model fits well with what we have said about our organization as a social system. Again, a system is identified by unity of purpose and interdependence of parts. We need one another to succeed. The lone ranger is doomed to die!

Jethro's Advice

An ant colony thrives because every ant does the job assigned it. Each has a function to perform and performs it well. When people operate in the same way, they can be just as productive. It's gratifying to see different people performing different tasks, all doing the jobs best suited for them. Every effort is coordinated toward the achievement of common goals.

In Exodus 18 Moses' father-in-law, Jethro, saw a problem with Moses' leadership style. Moses, assuming that he was indispensable, had succumbed to a common delusion of many leaders: unless they do it, it won't get done. Although Moses had a keen sense of responsibility, it expressed itself in total control. He had his finger in everything. Effective leaders keep their hands *on* everything, but not *in* everything. They have adequate systems in place to keep abreast of what's going on in the organization, but they do not seek to micromanage every decision. We must be able to train and then trust our associates as we give them decision-making powers to do their jobs effectively.

Moses' leadership style was ineffective for two reasons. First, he was doing himself and his family a disservice. Jethro pointed out that his son-in-law was burning himself out by working from "morning until evening" (verse 13, NKJV) and neglecting his family in the process. He had already sent them to live with Jethro (verse 2). Now Jethro was bringing them back to Moses (verses 5, 6).

Untold numbers of homes have fallen apart because of Christian leaders' obsession with their call. Many zealous denominational employees mistakenly assume that their families will always be there, because they understand the importance of the work they are doing. In a heart-to-heart visit many Christian leaders will tell of their private pain as they have seen their children drift from church and God. While every person is individually accountable for their response to the claims of the gospel, yet less-than-acceptable performance in our role as parents may influence the outcome for our children. Our first challenge as Christian leaders is to minister to our families. We should place them on our schedules no less than we would any other member. Don't leave them for leftover time, for the committed worker won't have any of that. Satan's goal is to wear you out, to weigh you down with "stuff" that isn't necessarily sinful but drains you physically and emotionally. Then when you get home you will be no good to yourself or anybody else. Managing your agenda is your responsibility, not God's.

Leaders need to establish priorities and discipline themselves to live by them. Nobody was more dedicated to God's work than Jesus, yet even He needed time alone with His Father. One of the first priorities set by the New Testament church leaders was to dedicate themselves to God's Word and prayer. We must learn: (a) what to do, (b) what to delegate, and (c) what not to pick up in the first place. Saying "I don't have time for my family" doesn't cut it. Everybody gets the same 24 hours to respond to either pressures or priorities. Decide what to set aside for now and what to unload for good. Don't get so involved with the work that you neglect your God or your family!

A second failure of Moses' leadership style was that he was wearing not only himself out, but the people as well (verse 18). Having everything go through him stifled initiative and caused resentment. The same thing happens today. One conference placed all major decisions on hold for more than three months while the president was on an overseas itinerary! In another area a leader earned the reputation of taking micromanagement down to a new level. Indeed, some leaders micromanage every detail to the extent that associates almost need to seek approval to use the restroom. Insecure leaders are unwilling to let go. They frustrate their followers and impede the progress of their organizations, which can move only as fast as the leader. Effective leadership is not controlling people, but empowering and liberating them to function for the good of the organization.

Moses was denying others their opportunities to serve. Their abilities remained dormant while he was working himself to death. Israel was not benefiting from the multiplicity of gifts within its midst. How often our local church, our conference office, our school or college, remains stymied because a few people have hugged the leadership roles for years and just won't let go. They scare off potential leaders and intimate that everything would fall to pieces without them.

Jethro advised Moses to share responsibility. His advice was simple: delegate! Choose leaders to deal with the easier, routine decisions and reserve your energies for the more difficult, policy decisions. It is frustrating for employees to find themselves forced to spend hours in meetings, dealing with minor procedural details that could be more efficiently handled at another level. In one conference I attended monthly executive committee meetings from 9:00 a.m. to as late as 8:00 p.m. The decisions we made were definitely not commensurate to the time expended. Often a mere telephone call or e-mail might save the time and energy of several committee members.

Following Jethro's advice allowed Moses time for his family while ensuring that the people received the attention they deserved. It also facilitated the emergence of new leaders, who would then grow from the exposure to valuable experience. Delegation allowed for greater involvement and teamwork: "They will share it with you" (verse 22, NIV). It is possible that Joshua and Caleb were among those selected. What a loss it would have been if these leaders had not emerged! Thankfully, Moses exhibited the qualities of a great leader. Having become aware of his limitations, he accepted the counsel of his father-in-law. Israel was better led because its leader heeded advice and shared in administration.

Developer of People

The growth and development of people is the highest calling of leaders. All church leaders should ensure that they produce other leaders. As a leader you have not succeeded if you have not left successors—persons who can step into your role without the organization's skipping a heartbeat. There can be no adequate success without adequate succession. Another reason for developing others is the nature of today's global job market. Cross training has become a buzzword in performance management circles, especially given the realities of a transient workforce. It is less likely today that a person would stay 40 years in one position. Thus equipping others to fulfill a particular role is absolutely necessary. But the task of growing others is not restricted to training personal replacements. Growing people must be the goal of every effective leader in both the for-profit and the not-for-profit sectors. This means creating a climate that encourages people to discover their talents and gifts in a nurturing, supportive environment.

Every leader must, as a precursor to people development, appreciate others for who they are, believe that they want to do their best, and then praise them for their accomplishments. Be generous with your approbations and liberal with your praise. Cultivate a "you can do it" atmosphere. It's amazing what people can achieve when they know that a leader they admire believes in them. Remember the incredible effect when someone you respected communicated their belief in your potential despite your own self-doubts? Some leaders mistakenly believe that too much commendation "swells the head." Well, apparently no one has ever received excessive praise for their efforts, for I have never seen any swollen heads (except from accidents!).

Developing the skills and talents of those we lead requires ongoing training. Followers—whether they are our children, our students, our employees, or our church or committee members—need help to broaden their skills and perspectives. Most important, they require opportunities in which to grow. The responsibilities may be very simple at first, but advancing in complexity as they gain experience. I well remember my first experience delivering the Sabbath school secretary's report in my local church in Couva, Trinidad. Although I practiced for two entire weeks I was still trembling when I stood to make the presentation. I was scared to death! But success in that assignment prepared me for greater responsibilities.

It's a good idea to offer people a broad range of experiences. John Maxwell, in *Developing the Leaders Around You,* states that in his organization a three-year rule applies. It asks leaders to change a significant number of major responsibilities every three years in order to develop new skills. The practice in some congregations, in which elders and treasurers remain in office continuously for 10, 20, or 30 years, is not in the best interest of the church. Brother Cato, an elder in one of my churches in Trinidad, set a better example. Even though he was very experienced as a first elder, he would never stay in that office for more than two terms at a time. He would then serve as an associate elder, wholeheartedly supporting, guiding, and encouraging the new leader, until the church again needed him in the leading role.

At a recent evangelistic program in Atlanta, Georgia, a young man approached me. I did not recognize him at first, but he reminded me that he had been a member of my congregation more than 10 years earlier. He remembered my encouraging the congregation to invite him to serve on the nominating committee, and he became its secretary. That experience made such an impression on his young mind that he rededicated his life to Christ and later entered the ministry. He was now a ministerial intern participating in that Atlanta meeting. People thrive on encouragement. It's oxygen for their souls.

In *Principle-centered Leadership* Stephen Covey states that one of the eight characteristics of principle-centered leaders is that they believe in other people (p. 35). Failing to allow everyone, whatever their background, to contribute their best will impoverish the organization. Effective leaders encourage passion and talent in those around them.

Of course, some people may frustrate your best efforts at their development. Their attitudes often hurt rather than help the program. Some are good only at opposing every idea or suggestion introduced. Sometimes personal issues have given them a negative outlook. Others are gifted but have difficulty working in a team environment. No matter how great a player is, if they can't play with the team they won't help the organization, for a team that does not bond does not build. A person with limited talents but the right attitude is a better prospect for greater responsibilities than a highly gifted individual with a rotten outlook. Regrettably some people for this reason will never realize their full potential. When it comes to selecting leaders, the best advice is to select for attitude and train for skill.

Finally, Christian leaders should not be afraid to work with people whose only "fault" is that they are smarter than their supervisors! There seems to be a tendency for leaders to appoint those whose ability and expertise are beneath their own. What happens over time is that the newer leaders continue the downward spiral of selecting those less able than themselves. Thus the organization suffers from progressively weaker administration, all because of the insecurity of its leaders. If we continually elect to office people who are smaller than we are, the church will become a congregation of dwarfs! On the other hand, if we seek to choose the best talent available, we will truly be in the business of leadership development and, consequently, organizational development.

As we look to the future and the need to find leaders for the rapidly expanding program of the church, I am convinced that God will bring men and women with commitment, talent, and passion to the fore to carry forward His work. These new individuals will come with their ideas, their vision, and their sense of how God is guiding them and the institutions they lead. Current leaders will have to train, trust, and, eventually, get out of the way! We will also have to accept that our methods are not the only ways to do the business of the church. Exciting times lie ahead, and they will be especially so as the church becomes more inclusive, transparent, and responsive to the Spirit's leadings. Goodbye, lone ranger! Welcome to consultation, consensus, and teamwork!

QUESTIONS FOR DISCUSSION

1. Jethro advised Moses to share the leadership responsibilities. Does delegation come easy for you, or do you have a tendency to do it all? Do you fear that someone else will not do it as well as you can? If so, how should you deal with those fears?

2. Does your organization have a plan for leadership development? Would you support an initiative to train and trust other, perhaps less experienced, leaders and assign them increasingly key leadership roles?

3. Are you a good listener? Are you able and/or willing to alter your leadership behaviors based on the feedback you receive from others?

It's Time for Change

It's exciting to be a leader. To influence the direction of an organization, to make a difference in people's lives, to have the assurance that you are fulfilling God's purpose for your existence—all contribute to making you want to go to work every morning. But leaders do not experience such feelings every day. A leader is in the business of change, of guiding people from where they are now to an uncharted but hopefully desired future. This process of leading people, individually and organizationally, often produces various emotional reactions in followers, not all of them positive. Many days the road gets bumpy for the leader.

Someone has said that a call to Christian leadership should carry with it a surgeon general's warning: Leadership is hazardous to your health. Some days nothing will seem to go right. You find yourself faced with disagreements from colleagues. They will question and criticize your actions. Tensions and conflicts arise in various quarters until you wonder what you are doing in that job. Such days will test your ability to lead from a biblical perspective. A leader must be aware that dynamic change and organizational trauma are closely linked. In this chapter we will discuss the reasons people have for resisting change, and in the next, we will address the ways in which that resistance manifests itself in an organization.

Resistance to Change

In any situation various forces drive change as well as resist it. The resistance may range from active and determined opposition to passive resistance, or even intellectual assent without corresponding behavioral responses.

As a leader you have to accept that no matter what you do, some will always disagree with your action, your method, or just your style.

Some critics will merely talk, while others will orchestrate opposition against your leadership. The idea that if you are working for God, everybody will then love you and every day will be sunny is myopic, to say the least, for even Jesus had critics during His earthly ministry. John reminds us of the words of Jesus: "If the world hates you, keep in mind that it hated me first" (John 15:18, NIV).

A person may resist change for several reasons. A leader who understands them will be able to respond appropriately and in a manner that represents Christ. Let's look at five main factors motivating those who oppose change.

1. *The Fear Factor.* Fear arises in the minds of many at the very mention of the word "change." Change represents a giving up of the charted, the familiar, and the known for the uncharted, the unfamiliar, and the unknown. A sense of loss may form the basis for some resistance. But the fear factor is the dominant cause of active opposition to change. Change often happens during conditions of uncertainty and can itself create more feelings of uncertainty. Another reason for fear is a perceived threat to one's personal interests. People are likely to challenge any change that would adversely affect their status quo. Turkeys would never vote for the American Thanksgiving holiday! Emotional and longstanding fears, rather than rationality, may lie at the root of other objections. It is helpful to understand the root cause of a person's resistance.

When I served as educational superintendent in the South England Conference of the Seventh-day Adventist Church, I recommended the first non-White teacher to one of our schools. Some on the board fiercely opposed the name, but it was finally voted. A couple years later I visited the school and was chatting with the principal. He remarked that the teacher had worked out so well that I would now face equally determined opposition if I tried to move her. Those who had resisted the change had come to recognize that their fears were unfounded.

In dealing with active opposition, it is important for the leader to be aware of both the driving and resisting forces at work. Who is for the change and what is the strength of their support? Who is against the projected change and what is the strength of their support? Kurt Lewin's force-field analysis technique is helpful here (*Field Theory in Social Science*).

LEWIN'S DRIVING AND RESTRAINING FORCES IN CHANGE

Force-Field Analysis

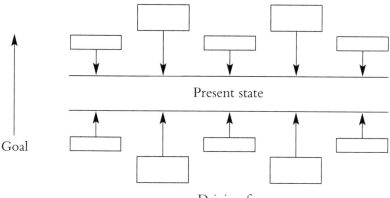

Restricting forces
Work on them to minimize and decrease them

Present state

Goal

Driving forces
Work on them to increase and strengthen them

In utilizing force-field analysis to develop a change strategy, we apply the following guidelines:

- If those who are for the change (the driving forces) far outweigh those who are against it (the restraining forces), then push on for the change.
- If the reverse is true—the restraining forces are much stronger than the driving forces—you have two choices:

    (1) give up the change effort, realizing that it will be too difficult to implement, or

    (2) pursue the change effort, concentrating on maintaining the driving forces while attempting either to immobilize each restraining force one by one or to transform it into a driving force.

- If the driving forces and restraining forces are fairly equal in a change situation, change agents will need to push the driving forces while at the same time attempting to convert or immobilize the restraining forces.

Thus if it is apparent that strong pockets of resistance to change exist because of the fear of the unknown or because of threats to members' or employees' self-interests or prestige, the leader will need to alter the resisting forces into driving forces for the change to succeed.

2. Complacency. Complacency is passive resistance resulting from a preference for stability and established habits and practices, and a desire to conform to tradition. The established ways bring a sense of security, for everyone knows what to expect. If anyone introduces anything divergent from the accepted norm, others will consider it disruptive. Inertia against change is especially likely when most perceive the organization as sailing smoothly. The approach of "it's not broken, why fix it" stalls any change efforts.

Lewin's three-step change process is particularly useful in overcoming inertia and effecting change. He described the three phases of the change process as unfreezing, changing, and refreezing. *Unfreezing* is a thawing process that leads people to question their present comforts or to perceive threats to those comforts. S. Vandermerwe and A. Vandermerwe ("Making Strategic Change Happen," *European Management Journal* 9, no. 2 [1991]: 174–181) refer to this step as creating *strategic discomfort.* Such discomfort seeks to make members deliberately yet constructively apprehensive about the organization's current position. The goal is to encourage them to think of the future and realize that without a major directional change, both the organization and their self-interests will be substantially and adversely affected. Visible crises arrest the attention of followers and create that discomfort that is a prelude to accepting change. The war on terror has made it possible for the U.S. government to introduce laws that intrude on personal privacy, and Americans have accepted them without much debate because of the perceived threats to national security.

Once individuals have become motivated to change, the second phase of the process is to provide them with new patterns of behavior. The process by which newly acquired behavior becomes integrated as patterned behavior in an individual's personality is referred to as *refreezing.* In the war on terror scenario, authorities highlighted threats to national security *(unfreezing),* introduced new laws and procedures *(change),* and encouraged the country to accept the new realities as a way of life for a secure future *(refreezing).* Our churches use a similar approach when we employ data to motivate people to stop smoking or to get off the couch and get some physical exercise.

But John Kotter points out that an organization must have leaders, not mere cautious managers, to overcome complacency. He argues that cautious managers will not push the urgency rate sufficiently high to effect a major transformation (*Leading Change,* pp. 43, 45). Actions that reduce complacency also tend to increase conflict and create tension. Thus leaders who always want to have people think well of them or are unduly concerned about maintaining a positive and successful image would not be the ones to raise the urgency level necessary to overcome complacency.

This issue of complacency is a major challenge facing the Seventh-day Adventist Church, especially in the developed countries. Comfortable, professional middle-class developed-country Christians are less likely to be passionate about witnessing and Christian service than people in developing countries. The figures for membership growth bear out this reality. Church growth theorists argue that the best prospects for conversion are people in some kind of emotional, political, economic, or social upheaval—in other words, those experiencing strategic discomfort.

3. Misperceptions. People may oppose change because they do not understand its implications and believe that it will cost them more than they will gain. Such a situation becomes worse when a lack of trust exists between the leader and the followers. Leaders held in suspicion by their followers will find it difficult to initiate any major change, for the followers will see the change as a means of getting something more out of them. That's why we have emphasized that a leader must have high credibility.

Another form of misperception concerns conflict in goals and expectations between the leaders and the led. The people's perceptions of a change may be quite different from those of the leaders', and the former may perceive more disadvantages than advantages, for both themselves and the organization. Such misperceptions give rise to suspicion, fear, or even open hostility. To overcome this form of resistance, leaders need to allow time and opportunity for the followers to discuss the potential change, and the leaders must make themselves available to clarify the advantages and respond to any misgivings that followers may have. While leaders may never reduce this form of resistance down to zero, by allowing time they go a long way toward minimizing its impact.

4. Timing. Change may also encounter resistance simply because it is rushed. A new idea springs to life in some boardroom or conference office and gets swiftly translated into organizational policy: "This is the way we are going to do it from now on." We must allow time for the idea to move from the minds of its originators to the minds of those that it will affect. Sometimes the volume, complexity, and speed of change frustrate people, and they suffer from what we might term *change fatigue*. They find it too difficult to cope with many transformations, and so they slide into neutral. As a relatively new academic planning team at Walla Walla University, we came up with some great ideas for change on our campus; but our wise academic vice president recognized that the organization could deal only with so much change at a time. We therefore paced the process and deferred some of the ideas.

Timing is also vital from the standpoint of allowing people an opportunity to talk about and take ownership of the change. People value what they own. Therefore, we must permit opportunity for them to see the issues clearly and to help in the framing and implementing of the desired changes. Involving people in solving their own issues and problems requires that they stay with the problem for as long as it takes to engage the solution and cement the change in the organization's structures and systems.

An important factor in minimizing resistance to change, time both heals and reveals. Each situation will have its own time context, depending on the nature, scope, and complexity of the issues involved. The leader must subtly and gently permit people to see the alternatives to their present situation as nonthreatening, possible, and in their best interests. Several years ago I was pastoring in England when I encouraged the church board to unite with the world church and introduce the *Seventh-day Adventist Hymnal* for worship services. For many years the church had been using a British hymnal, and so their initial response was to resist the idea. But the board set a date nine months into the future for the official date to shift over to the new hymnal. During that period the music team prepared the church for the transfer by gradually introducing pieces from the new hymnal and then accelerating the frequency of usage as the date drew closer. The time span allowed the members to come to terms with the change, and it was successfully implemented as scheduled.

5. Technology. We live in the midst of a technological revolution, and the speed at which new equipment and gadgets appear on the market can be frightening. When I worked at the South England Conference office in Watford, England, the receptionist refused to learn the new computerized method for labeling envelopes. She insisted on using her tried and trusted method on a 1960s machine because she perceived that the new system would make her life more stressful. While the introduction of new technology actually makes life easier in most cases, the leader needs to deal sensitively with the fear surrounding such devices, along with the possible displacement of employees that could occur as a result of mechanization.

On the other hand, some oppose change because administration has mandated it without sufficient information, backup systems, or appropriate technology. Technology is used here in its broader organizational sense, referring to the way of doing things. For instance, a few years ago the United States government encouraged Americans to receive a flu vaccine, only to learn that the vaccine was in short supply. The implementers of the policy were understandably distressed because of the absence of logistical support for the decision.

Conclusion

People support what they help create. "Our goals" are good goals, whereas "your goals" are not necessarily good goals for us. In overcoming resistance to change, therefore, we must seek to get participants to "own" the change as something they need, want, and are happy to live with.

Leaders must not be afraid to confront the challenges of change. Resistance to it is an understandable phenomenon that we must always anticipate and manage. It is imperative that all who play a role in change and who would be affected by it should it fail must feel and appreciate the need for the change. If a change program has merit and is sensitively managed, resistance—whether from fear, complacency, misperceptions, timing, or technology—may be minimized and the change program successfully implemented.

QUESTIONS FOR DISCUSSION

1. Reflect on a talked-about change in your church, conference, or other organization. Are you for or against the proposed change? Explain the reasons for your views.

2. Dynamic change and emotional trauma are closely linked. How would a Christian leader lessen the trauma associated with organizational change?

3. How could you prepare your committee, board, and/or constituency to accept a desired change?

11

When the Road
Gets Bumpy

In the previous chapter we discussed the resistance that we can expect when leading a change initiative. Now we will consider the fallout that the leader must deal with. We understand that the church is both a spiritual organism and a human organization. People who agree on the spiritual mission of the church may differ on approaches and methods. Even those on the same team will have different ideas as to the best strategy. The first lesson that Christian leaders must learn is that disagreements are likely, acceptable, and healthy. It is not correct to think that because we all love the Lord we will never have any disagreements. This realization is basic to understanding the dynamics involved in working with an organization.

Disagreements Are Healthy

Disagreements are not necessarily unhealthy. Indeed, an organization should welcome them. If everyone on a committee agrees on all the issues presented, it probably has an unbalanced membership. It is the mix and interchange of differing ideas that leads to strong, defensible decisions. We should fear the tendency to "groupthink" on our boards and committees. Oneness of mission and purpose must not lead to sameness of thought. Regrettably, some leaders regard any differing opinion among their subordinates as a sign of disloyalty. I have seen occasions on which administrators questioned committee members' motives and loyalties simply because they dared to differ with the leaders. Furthermore, colleagues would distance themselves from anyone whom they perceived to be "rocking the groupthink boat." A secure leader does not feel threatened by a different viewpoint, but welcomes it as assisting the group in arriving at a better decision.

On the other hand, some, in order to avoid all dissent, stifle their opinions. Because of their passive, noncritical approach, such yes-men and women get regarded as loyal subjects and are well received and long-serving in the organization. But the response actually weakens the institution, because, while it has extra hands and feet, it is bereft of the ideas and perspectives that those with different viewpoints could bring it.

Often, however, while such apparent loyalists do not speak up when it matters or could make a difference, they sulk at water fountains or behind closed doors or they underperform or undermine the organization because they are unhappy with the decisions made. One elected church leader refused to become involved with anything controversial. He was a no-show on big issues and justified his behavior as "a desire to be peaceful." But for any relationship to be healthy, all parties must respect and encourage alternative views in a safe, secure, nonthreatening climate of trust and Christlike acceptance. The popular concept of unity is a fantasy land in which disagreements never surface and contrary opinions never get stated. But there is nothing wrong with colleagues having alternative opinions. In fact, we ought to welcome them. So instead of talking about building unity, let's focus on building community.

While disagreements are healthy, we need to manage them in order to avoid disharmony and eventual conflict within the organization. Part of that involves an understanding of the source(s) of dissent. People disagree for various reasons. They may be experiencing significant insecurity about how they stand within the community. Some may be seeking to heighten their image in response to real or perceived slights. Others may be struggling with inner emotional conflicts. Or they may just not understand what you are trying to accomplish. One day my African-American friend Professor Standley Gellineau was shopping in a plaza off Interstate 90 in Montana. He approached the counter with his items, and the Caucasian female attendant inquired if he was a truck driver. Standley's race-awareness antenna shot way up as he blurted out, "Why did you ask me if I am a truck driver?"

"Because all truck drivers receive a discount at this store," the woman replied. Sometimes a leader may encounter much displeasure simply because the followers don't understand what he or she is trying to accomplish.

Dealing With Criticism

The apostle Paul gave some valuable counsel to Timothy on how to deal with those holding a different opinion. The *Message* paraphrase puts 2 Timothy 2:24, 25, this way: "God's servant must not be argumentative, but a gentle listener and a teacher who keeps cool, working firmly but patiently with those who refuse to obey. You never know how or when God might sober them up with a change of heart and a turning to the truth" (Message).

Christian leaders must handle criticism in a way that glorifies God and enables them to retain a redemptive concern for the critics. Whenever we are up front, people are going to take shots at us. No leader is exempt. The only way to avoid criticism is to say nothing, do nothing, be nothing—and even that isn't foolproof.

Nehemiah needed thick skin as a leader to deal with the criticisms he encountered when he went to restore the walls of Jerusalem. Fortunately he had it. "But when Sanballat, Tobiah, and Geshem the Arab heard of our plan, they scoffed contemptuously" (Neh. 2:19, NLT). Scoffing or mocking means "to utter repeatedly words of criticism." Add the word "contemptuously," and you get a picture of a real war of words! The criticisms continued throughout the entire building project, and even after its completion. But Nehemiah stuck to his task:

"Sanballat and Geshem sent this message: 'Come and meet with us at Kephirim in the valley of Ono.' I knew they were scheming to hurt me so I sent messengers back with this: 'I'm doing a great work; I can't come down. Why should the work come to a standstill just so I can come down to see you?'" (Neh. 6:2, 3, Message).

Here are seven ways to handle criticism, adapted from "Building Church Leaders," an online leadership journal published by *Christianity Today*:

1. Anticipate specific criticism. A capable leader knows the thought leaders in a group and often enlists their input and support before a meeting. Hearing the criticism in advance should help to refine your own thinking and make you aware of potential pitfalls.

2. Assume the criticism is logical. It's always best to regard a person's criticism as sincere. Given the base from which the person is working, the criticism may be entirely logical. The key is to understand others' beliefs, biases, experiences, theological positions, and especially their ego positions. Often their criticisms may have nothing to do with you personally, but rather reflect inner issues of failure and hurt.

3. Balance the criticism you receive. Leaders must know how to separate the criticism they receive from reality. One critical person may keep you from recognizing the hundred who agree. We should not mistake a vocal minority for a majority.

4. *Make constructive criticism part of the culture.* Since criticism is sure to come, it pays to make the constructive version a part of the established, understood organizational culture. This won't increase the amount of criticism—instead, it will channel it so that it benefits the organization.

5. *Don't turn criticism into a personal contest.* Often, if left alone, criticism will die of its own lack of meaning. Be willing to lose a battle in order to win a war. Some leaders are so insecure that they waste a lot of energy trying to squash every criticism. Like Nehemiah, we must learn not to react to all the criticisms leveled at us. Assess what needs a response and what we should let die a natural death.

6. *Admit when you've been wrong.* Consider every reasonable criticism as a chance to review your position. While the Scriptures might be inerrant, those of us who lead are not infallible.

7. *Don't take revenge.* It's important to personify tolerance and avoid all retribution. Some Christian leaders have been quite vindictive. One conference president had a reputation of banishing anyone who challenged his leadership to the remotest parts of his territory. Other leaders would refuse to speak with a colleague whom they believed may have spoken ill of them. But it is a sign of Christian maturity to live out the principles of the Beatitudes of Matthew 5: "Blessed are ye, when men shall revile you, and persecute you, and shall say all manner of evil against you falsely, for my sake. Rejoice, and be exceeding glad: for great is your reward in heaven: for so persecuted they the prophets which were before you. Ye are the salt of the earth" (verses 11-13).

Theodore Roosevelt said: "It is not the critic who counts; not the man who points out how the strong man stumbles or where the doer of deeds could have done them better. The credit belongs to the man who is actually in the arena, whose face is marred by dust and sweat and blood; who strives valiantly; who errs, and comes up short again and again, because there is not effort without error and shortcoming; but who does actually strive to do the deed; who knows the great enthusiasms, the great devotions; who spends himself in a worthy cause; who at the best knows in the end the triumph of high achievement, and who at the worst, if he fails, at least fails while daring greatly."

"Far better it is to dare mighty things, to win glorious triumphs; even though checkered by failure, than to take rank with those poor spirits who neither enjoy much nor suffer much, because they live in the gray twilight that knows not victory nor defeat."

Dealing With Conflict

Britannica Online describes the word "conflict" as "a struggle resulting from incompatible or opposing needs, drives, wishes, or demands." Wherever people come together, whether in the home, the church, the workplace, or any community association, conflict is likely to be present. We all think differently, and when our differences preclude agreement on a path forward, dissension may arise.

Here are seven guidelines for dealing with such conflict:

1. *Attend to it immediately and personally.* Don't save up all your complaints and problems to dump on the critic in one fell swoop.

2. *Confront with the right spirit.* "Let this mind be in you, which was also in Christ Jesus" (Phil. 2:5).

3. *Start on a positive note.* Seek to preserve the other person's sense of well-being. In dealing with their children's conflicts, James Dobson counsels parents to shape the will but do not break the spirit.

4. *Outline the nature of the conflict as you see it.* Speak in the first person as much as possible. Describe what is being done, how it makes you feel, and why you desire a change.

5. *Encourage a response.* Accept that you don't know everything. Show willingness to listen to another viewpoint. Adopt the attitude that the other person is an ally, not an enemy.

6. *Mutually seek a win/win resolution.* Remember, leadership is about relationship.

7. *Bury the hatchet once the problem has been dealt with.* Do not bring it up again unless the problem recurs or you can use it to affirm positive change and growth.

Confrontation

Part of the process of developing others is evaluating their performance. It is easier to offer praise and compliments than it is to tell someone they have not lived up to expectations. Generally we do not like confrontation. Some leaders fear to meet issues head-on because they wish to be seen as "Mr. Nice Guy" or "Ms. Friendly," and saying what needs to be said may tarnish that image. Others fear that confrontation may worsen the problem by leading to anger, dislike, or rejection from the person being dealt with. But when a person's behavior is inappropriate, failing to challenge the individual about it only worsens the situation for the future.

If secretaries do not do their job, the church or department suffers.

Such disorganization reflects negatively on me as church pastor or department head. But unchecked poor performance also hurts the secretaries, because they do not receive an opportunity to recognize their deficiencies and grow from them. I have therefore robbed them of a chance to develop their stewardship potential. By refusing to address unacceptable work, the organization injures itself. Whenever leaders fail to deal honestly and caringly with underperformance, they need to ask themselves: Did I remain silent for my own benefit or the other person's? If it was for your own benefit, then you are being selfish and political, for you are seeking to buy that person's goodwill at the expense of both your and their personal, professional, and even spiritual development.

Several years ago I had to deal with Jim (not his real name), an underperforming teacher. Jim was the nicest Christian you ever met. He was ready and willing to attend to everybody's needs, but he unfortunately often did so at the expense of his own commitments. It was not unusual for him to arrive late and unprepared for his classes because he had been helping somebody else. I attended the same church with him, where he was also known for being late to meetings and appointments. Although I had been the beneficiary of his kindness in the past, I could not allow his tardiness and lack of class preparation to go unchecked. Following due process, I began with an informal talk, followed by a letter, and then a second letter. But Jim's work did not improve. He always had an excuse for his underperformance or his failure to meet agreed-upon targets.

After a few more attempts, including assistance from the church pastor, I finally recommended to the board the termination of Jim's contract. One member commented that it was perhaps the first time that anyone had held Jim accountable for his tardiness and lack of preparation. He had gone through life with a warm smile, expecting everyone to overlook his weaknesses. Regrettably, he did not respond to counsel, and became quite bitter over the decision of the school board. But as leaders, we do not help someone if we fail to hold them accountable. Hopefully, in most cases of confrontation, a more positive result will emerge.

Confrontation can be a positive experience if entered into with the goal of achieving a win/win situation. We must see it as an opportunity to develop a colleague. Thus we should never challenge in anger or hurl invectives at the other person. Never approach anyone in such a way as to demonstrate your power or to crush your hapless victim. Please confront with respect, for you are dealing with another human being—God's precious heritage. Your intent must be to seek the other person's best interest. John Maxwell lists 10 guidelines for win/win situations:

1. Confront as soon as possible after the incident warranting it.
2. Separate the person from the wrong action.
3. Confront only what the person can change.
4. Give the person the benefit of the doubt.
5. Be specific.
6. Avoid sarcasm.
7. Avoid words such as "always" and "never."
8. Tell the person how you feel about what was done wrong.
9. Give the person a game plan to fix the problem.
10. Affirm him or her as a person and a friend.

(Adapted from *Developing the Leaders Around You*, pp. 126-128.)

Conclusion

A call to Christian leadership is a demanding one. It is a summons to reflect the principles of Christ as you lead your organization into the future. Reflecting Christian principles when you have been hurt or when someone has used or abused you is not easy. But your effectiveness lies in your ability to retain your grace and your Christianity both in the sunshine and in the shadows of life. The Christian never has any excuse to act in an unchristian manner, especially the Christian leader. Yes, the road will get bumpy at times. And yes, you will find yourself tempted to get down in the quagmire with your detractors, but Christ says to you in those moments: "My grace is sufficient for you" (2 Cor. 12:9, NKJV). Keep your focus, keep your faith, and keep following in the path of our Lord, who modeled for all of us selfless, sacrificial servant leadership.

QUESTIONS FOR DISCUSSION

1. What is, and what should be, your attitude toward those who have a different opinion from yours?

2. One of your assistants constantly turns in substandard performances. Should you address the issue? do nothing about it? keep your frustration to yourself or to a few trusted workmates? wait for an opportunity to terminate the person? Discuss the reasons for your answer.

3. As an associate in the organization, you are unhappy that its leader makes unilateral decisions. What should you do?

A Case Study
in Christian Leadership

Be a Leader!

My most exciting challenge as a church leader came when I served as the principal of an inner-city high school in London, England: the John Loughborough Seventh-day Adventist School.

The institution had an interesting history. With the arrival in England of the ship S.S. *Empire Windrush* from Jamaica in 1948, Black Britain was born in earnest. The flow of Caribbean immigrants continued from that time and included many Seventh-day Adventist believers. They brought not only their religion but also their church's passion for Christian education. When the education commitment coupled with the problems that Black Adventist children encountered in British classrooms, it created momentum for a Seventh-day Adventist church school in London. The desire of the Black members did not meet an immediate willing response from the indigenous church hierarchy, but they persisted, and the school formally opened on April 5, 1980.

Cecil Perry, an early Caribbean minister who later became president of the British Union, wrote that "the establishment of the John Loughborough School was seen by our members as the focal point of collective effort. It was a rallying point—the act of being heard. In a sense it was like a coming into nationhood, galvanizing the various streams of the immigrant community. It also sent a message to the rest of the British church" (quoted in C. Valley, "Managing Change in the Seventh-day Adventist Church: An Interpretative Study on the Establishment of The John Loughborough School").

During the more than a quarter century of its existence, the school has attracted a great deal of media attention for its standards of discipline, the academic achievements of its students, and its strong Christian ethos. Many television and radio documentaries and newspaper articles featured the school as a bastion of hope for London's Black and Asian community. It is referred to in the halls of academia and referenced in the literature on British education. A former principal has been toasted at 10 Downing Street, the official residence of the British prime minister. The school is therefore seen as a successful experiment, particularly in the education of Black and other ethnic minority youngsters, and its impact in the country far outstrips its modest annual enrollment of 300 students.

I was principal of the school when on September 1, 1998, after a 10-year struggle, it received approval from the British Labor government for funding as a grant-maintained school. The church community saw the decision as a significant victory for parental choice. Their children now had access to a quality Christian education with financial support from the central government. At the same time, the church retained overall control of the school, and the president of the South England Conference remained chair of its Board of Governors.

My coming to the school was rather providential. Having served as the education superintendent of the South England Conference for six years, I had accepted an invitation to work in the Caribbean in April 1993. While there my son fell ill, and physicians advised us to return to England for his medical care. Meanwhile the principal at John Loughborough had been promoted to my former position, thereby creating a vacancy at the school. In my eagerness to return with my family to England, I took up the challenge at the school eight months after I had left for the Caribbean.

I say challenge, for indeed it was! The school was going through a difficult period. Enrollment had declined, academic standards were low, the financial picture was bleak, and staff morale was low. On my first day on the job a bank manager called to share some depressing news. The conference treasurer indicated that the school had no more than six months before closure. One concerned friend, when he heard of my new assignment, wondered whether I needed medical certification (a British term for being declared insane). Another lamented that I had drunk from the poisoned chalice. However, it seemed that through my background, training, and experience, God had been preparing me to lead the turnaround of His school.

I saw my task as unraveling a knotted length of organizational thread. It would require patience, skill, and sensitivity. One by one we worked on the knots at John Loughborough, and they began to loosen. Mini-victories gave both a sense of relief and a spur to further efforts and attainments. Prior to state funding, the school's enrollment stabilized around 140 students, but it immediately doubled to more than 300 at the onset of grant-maintained status. The financial position went from red to black, and the academic achievements of students as reflected in the national league tables almost quadrupled, advancing from 11 percent to a high of 41 percent. All these results were the collective achievements of a revitalized faculty and staff and the prayerful support of the church constituency.

We also had our difficult days. As we built for the future, we had to find a common path amid varied and sometimes conflicting personalities and interests. Regrettably, it produced some pain, for staff reductions were unavoidable. Further, not everyone fully understood or agreed on the vision for the future. Change is difficult, and no matter how gradual the process or how clearly you seek to communicate its necessity, some remain cemented to the status quo. Thankfully, the majority of parents, staff, board members, and the Seventh-day Adventist constituency remained supportive. My role was principally that of cheerleader, encouraging flagging spirits and removing roadblocks in the paths of successful efforts.

Leadership is primarily a matter of influence. The leader is the conductor of the orchestra, ensuring that the various specialists harmonize their individual efforts into a beautiful piece of music. The skills of the leader are *process* skills rather than *content* skills. Conductors may not be expert on any of the instruments, but they have a sense of what constitutes good music and are able to pull this together from the skills of the players. Leaders work with the compliant and the defiant, the bright stars and the lesser mortals, striving to understand them all, to operate within the context of their needs and to motivate them to pull together for the sake of the team. Secure in themselves and having a clear sense of the desired end, such leaders are able to chart a course into that new reality. Here is the role of a leader. This approach has worked for me as a pastor, as principal at John Loughborough School, and more recently as an administrator at Walla Walla University.

The General Conference administration is highlighting the need for a new breed of leaders because of the expected growth and increasing complexity of the world church. Emphasizing the need for visionary leadership for the new era, Jan Paulsen, world president, made the following remarks in his presentation during the Profiling Adventist Leadership presentations at the 2005 General Conference session:

"Vision is the capacity to see beyond where you are presently standing—to see the opportunities, and define their values. Leadership that lacks vision is at best managerial only. Looking to its leadership, the Seventh-day

Adventist community wants to know where they are going, not just what they hold in their hands."

He also spoke of the need to focus on the mission of the church.

"An Adventist leader, at the local church as well as at other levels of organization, will, and must ever be, very deliberate in focusing the church on mission. Mission is the environment in which the church comes alive. A leader who cannot, or will not, see this should not carry a leadership assignment. Let it be clear: Mission is *the* primary reason for our being as a church."

This emphasis on visionary, mission-focused leaders is a healthy sign, for the church has had a tendency in the past to appoint longstanding loyalists without regard, necessarily, for their visionary leadership ability. There seemed to be a bias for "incumbency" appointments, people who have worked their way up the ladder merely on the basis of longevity. I have sensed an aversion for hiring from outside the local organization's network or, worse yet, from among Seventh-day Adventists outside the denominational system. But such an approach closes the door on a number of excellent personnel resources. God uses a variety of means to prepare workers for His cause, and our selection committees need to remain open and responsive to His leading—whether it is to someone inside the organization or to one from the wider world church family.

I argue for a system that makes personnel decisions based on a meritocracy model rather than one built merely on longevity. Every vacancy is another window of hope for the organization. It is an opportunity to rethink mission, reassess priorities, and review the position's requirements in the light of the present realities. Having completed such an analysis, the selection committee can then decide what the organization best needs at that time. With this information the hiring process ought to bring to the fore the best in line, not merely the next in line—as our current system seems to favor. I appreciate the leadership at Walla Walla University for being open when considering me for my current position. When first approached, I reacted skeptically, for I knew absolutely nobody from that part of the country. I felt sure that some insider had the edge, yet the institution offered me the position despite the fact that I was an outsider, and what a valuable and enjoyable experience it has been!

If we wish to see a new generation of creative, visionary, mission-focused leaders for our church, then the selection criteria for leadership roles should be based on the personal specifications that make for effective leadership rather than merely on how well known or well connected the candidates are.

We cannot afford mere pen-pushing bureaucrats whose main goal is to get through the day without any major conflict. For too many in leadership positions the name of the game is survival. They occupy the office, drawing their paychecks, but they are not really making a difference in their organizations. It is difficult to find significant achievements that one could point to as trophies of their tenure. Such employees are simply treading water.

Henry and Richard Blackaby put it this way:

"When an organization continually struggles, when it regularly loses to the competition, when no new ideas are being generated, when key personnel are leaving, when morale is chronically low, when there is no exciting anticipation for the future—these are all indications that something needs to change. Either the leader needs a dramatic turnaround, or the time has come for a new leader with different skills to take charge" (*Spiritual Leadership*, p. 257).

Lackluster nonvisionary leaders must bear the responsibility for their organizations falling into that pitiable state of having plans without purpose, meetings without meaning, and activity without productivity. At such times somebody needs to call them to accountability. A discussion must start as to whether it is best for them and the organization for them to be trained, transferred, or terminated. Leaders must do more than plug a gap. They must be visionaries who make significant differences in their departments, churches, or institutions.

Please note also that the role of leader is distinct from that of follower. Being the main follower does not equip you to be the leader, for the leadership skill set is quite specific and different. An excellent personal assistant would not necessarily make a great CEO. My assistant, Bev, and I make a great team. I believe she thinks so as well. Bev is great in detail, in organizing, in controlling, in budgeting—in short, she is an excellent manager. On the other hand, I love the big-picture thinking, the visioning, and the strategic planning. At times I raise her blood pressure with my out-of-the-box concepts, but I need her skills in adding form and structure to my ideas.

Organizations need visionary presidents working with executive secretaries and/or treasurers who have strong managerial skills. That is a winning team! But an executive secretary should only be promoted to president if that person has big-picture visioning skills—not merely because he or she was next in line.

In England people refer to the school principal as the head teacher. But that is a misnomer, for the position of teaching is a different job altogether

111

from leadership of the school. While background experience is important and will influence a person's judgment, the leader's prime expertise now must not focus on a specific area of professional competence but on the dynamics of leadership. A leader's role is not to be the super teacher or super pastor or super employee, but to recruit and retain excellent personnel who will help fulfill the vision of the organization. Many heads of organizations make the sad mistake of trying to do what others should be doing, forgetting that they have been called to lead. While leadership does involve modeling and getting one's hands dirty as part of the team, yet if the leader is merely functioning as another employee, then who is doing the leading?

Ultimately, Christian leadership is about preparing people for a better, more satisfying life, both now and eternally. Whether we are working with children, young people, or adults; whether we are in a school, a church, or another area of service, our main task is to prepare people "for the joy of service in this world and for the higher joy of wider service in the world to come" (*Education*, p. 13). As Seventh-day Adventist leaders, this is what we believe. It's exciting to guide others to a better, richer, more fulfilling way of life, now and eternally. This fills me with the greatest satisfaction and meaning. Do you share that perspective?

QUESTIONS FOR DISCUSSION

1. **Discuss the merits and demerits** of the leadership behaviors and decisions adopted by the author in his case study.

2. **The John Loughborough School** had to make some difficult decisions, and some staff members lost their jobs. How should we balance the needs of the organization with those of individuals in it?

3. **List some strategies you find helpful in dealing with critics.**

Epilogue

This book has addressed principles of Christian leadership with particular reference to leadership within the Seventh-day Adventist Church. It is one of the fastest growing Christian denominations, particularly in the developing world. We rejoice at the success of evangelistic initiatives such as the Net programs, Global Outreach efforts, and the Sow One Billion plan. The Lord has blessed our health and educational systems, our various ministries, and the programs of ADRA International. The reports of recent General Conference sessions make us proud to be part of a growing, thriving movement that is under the guidance of the Spirit of God.

But the years ahead will be challenging for Christians and the Christian church, and we as Seventh-day Adventists are not immune to the various issues. We will face changing realities, emphases, and demands. Globalization, urbanization, technological advancements, diversity issues, growing religious apathy, rampant materialism, and similar forces will make new demands upon our organization. I therefore applaud the focus on leadership development, for so much will hang or fall on leadership in this new era.

But leadership development will require accompanying organizational development. It must be part of a cultural transformation within the church structure as we seek to remain relevant and effective in the twenty-first century. Furthermore, we must see leadership development as necessary not only for people new to the leadership role, but for all our present leaders. Thus while we may provide short one-, two- or three-day seminars for leaders, we need to regard them as just a small part of an overall process of ongoing growth for all leaders in the church. Lifelong learning must become the buzzword in this new culture. To survive and thrive in the new world environment requires flexibility from all of us, both individually and organizationally. This necessitates constant learning.

As members of the body of Christ, we will constantly need to reexamine our faith in the changing circumstances and reinterpret it in the light of new paradigms. We have already seen the need for the addition of a twenty-eighth fundamental doctrine, and it may not be the last. I am not suggesting any new truths, but rather a better way of clarifying what we hold precious in the light of new realities. What must be paramount is a personal, abiding communion with Christ. While doctrines may be refined, reinterpreted, or better understood, Christ is the way who leads always and only into all truth. Such a relationship enables the Christian to respond as Jesus would to issues and conflicts for which we have no precedents, for it is "not I, but Christ [that] liveth in me: and the life which I live now in the flesh I live by the faith of the Son of God" (Gal. 2:20).

As Christian leaders, let us encourage our members to develop a personal relationship with Christ and to depend on Him rather than on us or the organizations we head. Christ is the supreme leader of His church, and we all are to follow only as He directs. My first assignment as a young ministerial intern was at the Stanmore Avenue church in Port of Spain, Trinidad. The senior pastor at that time was Fitzgerald Harris. I remember him saying to me during our first visit together: "Clinton, in the ministry, the brethren would ask you to take on several assignments and pull you in all directions. But while you are directed by the brethren, be led by the Lord!"

On a corporate level, the church will have to continue nurturing a culture that facilitates change. E. M. Schein contrasted two organizational cultures in this way: organization A has a hush in the air. Everyone is in an office with closed doors. Nothing gets done except by appointment or prearranged agenda. When people of different ranks gather, they do so in deference and obedience. An air of formality permeates everything. On the other hand, in organization B we find open offices, few closed doors, people milling about, intense conversations and disagreement, and a general air of informality ("Coming to a New Awareness of Organizational Culture," *Sloan Management Review*, 1984). Which organization will likely cope better with change?

The church that will survive and thrive in the twenty-first century will be the one that allows its functions to determine its form, not vice versa. Structure will be subservient to mission, facilitating rather than hindering it. It will be a church that emphasizes people above policies; process above product; and mission above money. Such a church encourages talent and expertise above loyalty and longevity; will be as eager to protect the rights of individuals as it is its good name; will be all-inclusive and recognize that all God's children—irrespective of age, gender, ethnicity, or personal connections—are equals; will offer everyone the same privileges and opportunities to function, to witness, and to glorify the name of God through the use of their God-given talents and abilities; and will be a church in which leaders do not fear frontline ministry and conference officials do not regard it a demotion to be called to full-time pastoral and evangelistic ministry. Servant leaders do not see promotions or demotions—only different areas of service.

The effective twenty-first-century church will be one that plans proactively and with vision for the unentered future, yet pauses to evaluate critically past performances, seeking to learn from former mistakes—yes, mistakes—rather than covering them in the garb of mystical infallibility. It will be a church that daily incarnates the Christ who went about doing good and never feared to confront sin. Finally, it will be a church in which leaders keep their focus on mission, rather than on status, trips, and the perks of position. Their prime emphasis will be on the Savior, not the salary; on service, not the sustentation package; on sacrifice, not selfish indulgence. We must ever remember that our model is the lowly Galilean, for whom "foxes have holes and birds of the air have nests, but the Son of Man has nowhere to lay his head" (Matt. 8:20, NKJV).

In sum, the effective Seventh-day Adventist Christian Church in the twenty-first century will be a body of believers whose members and leaders will be close to Christ, close to one another, committed in their lifestyle, singular in their mission, and eager in their anticipation for the return of their coming Lord. Even now, I pray that this may be a reality for my church.

Ellen G. White
on Christian Leadership

In 1985 the Board of Trustees of the Ellen G. White Estate published a series of quotations from Ellen White in a book entitled Christian Leadership. Reprinted in September 1995, it is available from the Ellen G. White Estate in Silver Spring, Maryland. With the permission of the White Estate, I include here some of those quotations.

Christian Leadership

Christian Leadership—Praying Leadership—. . . . But they are to see in every difficulty a call to prayer.—*Prophets and Kings*, p. 31.

Responsibility of Leadership No Child's Play—. . . . In that important position God will have a man to venture, to risk something; to move out firmly for the right, whatever may be the consequences; to battle against obstacles, and waver not, even though life be at stake.—*Testimonies*, vol. 1, p. 320.

Pleasure in Bruising Souls—I am sorry that there are those in positions of trust who very sparingly cultivate the sympathy and tenderness of Christ. They do not even cultivate and manifest love toward their brethren and sisters who are in the faith.—Letter 43, 1895, p. 3 (June 14, 1895, to J. H. Kellogg).

Unfaithfulness to Be Disapproved—. . . . Never are God's servants to look upon disaffection, scheming, and deception as virtues; those in responsibility are to manifest their decided disapproval of all unfaithfulness in business and spiritual matters.—*Review and Herald*, Sept. 14, 1905.

Humility

Haphazard Leadership—You love praise and excitement and to bring yourself to the front. You care far more for the approbation and praise of men then for the approval of God.—Letter 3, 1882, p. 3 (Apr. 1, 1882).

God Exalts the Humble—He is most fit to carry responsibilities and command who most resembles God in character.—Letter 39, 1898, p. 13 (March 27, 1898, to Brethren Woods and Miller).

Time for a Change—. . . When men feel that their ideas are without a flaw, it is time for them to change their position from president to that of a learner. When they think that their ideas, their judgment, should be accepted without question, they show that they are unfit for their position.—Manuscript 55, 1897 (June 3, 1897, "Development of Workers").

Position Does Not Give Holiness—. . . It is by honoring God and obeying His commands that a man is made truly great. . . . So long as he remains consecrated, the man who God has endowed with discernment and ability will not manifest an eagerness for high position, neither will he seek to rule or control.—*Prophets and Kings*, pp. 30, 31.

Leaders Are Learners—Those who accept a position of responsibility in the cause of God should always remember that with the call to this work God has also called them to walk circumspectly before Him and before their fellow men. Instead of considering it their duty to order and dictate and command, they should realize that they are to be learners themselves. When a responsible worker fails to learn this lesson, the sooner he is released from his responsibilities the better it will be for him and for the work of God. Position never will give holiness and excellence of character. He who honors God and keeps His commandments is himself honored.

The question which each should ask himself in all humility is: "Am I qualified for this position? Have I learned to keep the way of the Lord to do justice and judgment?" The Savior's earthly example has been given us that we should not walk in our own strength, but that each should consider himself, as Solomon expressed it, "a little child."—*Testimonies*, vol. 9, pp. 282, 283.

Cultivate Humble Dependence—Men whom the Lord calls to important positions in His work are to cultivate a humble dependence upon Him.—*Testimonies*, vol. 9, p. 270.

Integrity

No Underhanded Dealings—Do nothing in an underhanded manner; be open as the day, true to your brethren and sisters, dealing with them as you wish Christ to deal with you. If you had the Spirit of Christ, you would not notice slights and make much of fancied injuries.—*Review and Herald,* May 14, 1895.

Unbending Integrity—An honest man, according to Christ's measurement, is one who will manifest unbending integrity.—*Testimonies,* vol. 4, p. 310.

Confidence

The People Have Lost Confidence—. . . Yet we hear that the voice of the conference is the voice of God. Every time I have heard this, I have thought it was almost blasphemy. The voice of the conference ought to be the voice of God, but it is not, because some in connection with it are not men of faith and prayer, they are not men of elevated principle.— Manuscript 37, 1901, p. 8 (April 1901 talk by Mrs. E. G. White in the Review Chapel regarding the Southern work).

Influence

Influence Reflected in People—There is need of Nehemiahs in the church today—not men who can pray and preach only, but men whose prayers and sermons are braced with firm and eager purpose. . . . When they have laid their plans, they should present them to the church in such a manner as to win their interest and cooperation. Let the people have a personal interest in its prosperity. The success attending Nehemiah's efforts shows what prayer, faith, and wise, energetic action will accomplish.—*Christian Service,* p. 177.

Individuality

Individual Methods of Labor—The leaders among God's people are to guard against the danger of condemning the methods of individual workers who are led by the Lord to do a special work that but few are fitted to do. Let brethren in responsibility be slow to criticize movements that are not in perfect harmony with their methods of labor. . . . Let them not fear to trust another's methods; for by withholding their confidence from a brother laborer who, with humility and consecrated zeal, is doing a special work in God's appointed way, they are retarding the advancement of the Lord's cause.—*Testimonies,* vol. 9, p. 259.

Authority

A Council of Men—Not Just One Man—. . . In the work of God no kingly authority is to be exercised by any human being, or by two or three.—Manuscript 26, 1903 (Apr. 3, 1903, "Re: The Work of the General Conference").

Dealing With Men Like Ourselves—Let us all remember that we are not dealing with ideal men, but with real men of God's appointment, men precisely like ourselves, men who fall into the same errors that we do, men of like ambitions and infirmities.—Manuscript 29, 1907, pp. 9, 10 ("Individual Responsibility and Christian Unity," January 1907).

The Spirit of Authority—. . . A spirit of authority is not to be exercised, even by the president of a conference; for position does not change a man into a creature that cannot err.—Letter 10, 1903, pp. 3, 4 (Jan. 8, 1903, to E. R. Palmer and A. G. Daniells).

Dictatorship

How the Wheels of Progress Are Clogged—. . . They dismiss the Holy Spirit from their councils, and then, under the power and name of the General Conference, they invent regulations through which they compel men to be ruled by their own ideas and not by the Holy Spirit.—Letter 83, 1896 (May 22, 1896, to O. A. Olsen).

Leadership Is Not Lordship—I am instructed by the Lord to say that position never gives a man grace or makes him righteous. "The fear of the Lord is the beginning of wisdom." Some men entrusted with positions of responsibility entertain the idea that position is for the aggrandizement of self.—*Medical Ministry*, p. 165.

The Conference President—Again and again I repeat the warning: Never place as president of a conference a man who supposes that such a position gives him the power to dictate and control the consciences of others. It is natural for man to have a large estimate of self; old habits wrestle for the supremacy; but the man who occupies a position of trust should not glorify himself. . . . Never should he usurp authority, or command or threaten, saying, "Unless you do as I say, you will receive no pay from the conference." A man who would speak such words is out of his place as president of a conference.—Letter 416, 1907, pp. 5, 6 (Dec. 30, 1907, to A. G. Daniells and W. C. White).

Not to Control Other Men's Minds

Molding Other Men's Minds—How my heart aches to see presidents of conferences taking the burden of selecting those whom they think they can mold to work with them in the field. They take those who will not differ with them, but will act like mere machines. No president has any right to do this.—*Testimonies to Ministers*, p. 304.

Credit Others With Some Sense—. . . Men who follow the leading of another, and are willing that another should think for them, are unfit to be entrusted with responsibility. . . . Men in responsible positions should credit others with some sense, with some ability of judgment and foresight and look upon them as capable of doing the work committed to their hands.—Letter 12, 1885 (Oct. 28, 1885, To G. I. Butler and S. N. Haskell).

Teamwork

Place Responsibility on Others—. . . We want every responsible man to drop responsibilities upon others. Set others at work that will require them to plan, and to use judgment. Do not educate them to rely upon your judgment. Young men must be trained up to be thinkers.—*Testimonies to Ministers*, pp. 302, 303.

Let Others Learn to Bear Responsibilities—. . . He wants you to lay off work and be more a planner, a manager. . . . Will you heed advice? Will you let others learn to bear responsibilities even if they make blunders while you are a living man to show them how to work?—Letter 117, 1886, p. 6 (June 25, 1886, to G. I. Butler).

Duty to Train Others—. . . It is your duty to train others to stand in responsible positions that should you need a change and rest, which is your due, you can have it. . . . And again you have worked intensely upon the high pressure plan. God has spared your life, but you are not immortal, and you may die as others have died before you who have lived two years in one.—Letter 7, 1886 (Apr. 26, 1886, to J. H. Kellogg).

Wisdom From God to Be Interwoven in Daily Experiences—. . . The way to become great and noble is to be like Jesus, pure, holy, and undefiled. The honor that you may receive of medical and great men is not of much value as I view it, but the honor you receive of the Lord is of the greatest value.—Letter 7, 1886 (Apr. 26, 1886, to J. H. Kellogg).

No Kingly Authority in Seventh-day Adventist Church—God has not set any kingly power in the Seventh-day Adventist Church to control the whole body, or to control any branch of the work. He has not provided that the burden of leadership shall rest upon a few men. Responsibilities are distributed among a large number of competent men.—*Testimonies,* vol. 8, p. 236.

Decision-making

Hesitant Leadership Is Weak Leadership—It is even more excusable to make a wrong decision sometimes than to be continually in a wavering position; to be hesitating, sometimes inclined in one direction, than in another. More perplexity and wretchedness result from thus hesitating and doubting than from sometimes moving too hastily. . . .

God requires promptness of action. Delays, doubtings, hesitation, and indecision frequently give the enemy every advantage.—*Gospel Workers,* p. 134.

Choosing Personnel

Choose Men Who Have Experience in Faith—Those who are thus appointed as overseers of the flock should be men of good repute; men who give evidence that they have not only a knowledge of the Scriptures, but an experience in faith, in patience, that in meekness they may instruct those who oppose the truth. They should be men of thorough integrity, not novices, but intelligent students of the Word, able to teach others also, bringing from the treasure-house things new and old; men who in character, in words, in deportment, will be an honor to the cause of Christ, teaching the truth, living the truth, growing up to the full stature in Christ Jesus. This means the development and strengthening of every faculty by exercise, that the workers may become qualified to bear larger responsibilities as the work increases.—*Gospel Workers,* p. 413.

Training Leaders

Leaders Afraid to Train Others—If in their ministry those whom we teach develop an energy and an intelligence even superior to that which we possess, we should be led to rejoice over the privilege of having a part in the work of training them. But there is danger that some in positions of responsibility as teachers and leaders will act as if talent and ability have been given to them only, and that they must do all the work in order to make sure that it is done aright. They are liable to find fault with everything not originated by themselves. A great amount of talent is lost to the cause of God because many laborers, desiring to be first, are willing to lead, but never to follow. Although they closely scrutinize and criticize all that anyone else does, they are in danger of regarding that which goes forth from their hands as perfect.—*Review and Herald*, Dec. 1, 1904.

Recognize Talent—Those who are placed in responsible positions should feel it their duty to recognize talent. They should learn how to use men, and how to advise them.—Manuscript 55, 1897 (June 3, 1897, "Development of Workers").

Majoring in Minors

Counsel to a Leader—. . . You have, I have been shown, neglected large responsibilities while you bring your mind to embrace small matters which others could and should do equally as well as yourself. But the loss of a few pennies in any enterprise seems to you so large and would grieve you so sorely, that you feel that you must have everything under your inspection; therefore much good and great work is neglected for things of minor consequence.—Letter 40, 1879, pp. 1, 5.

Committee Meetings

Accountable to God—Let everyone who sits in council and committee meetings write in his heart the words, I am working for time and for eternity; and I am accountable to God for the motives that prompt me to action.—*Testimonies*, vol. 7, pp. 258, 259.

Trusting God

Trust God—Wait Patiently—. . . Despondency may shake the most heroic faith, and weaken the most steadfast will. But God understands, and He still pities and loves. He reads the motives and the purposes of the heart. To wait patiently, to trust when everything looks dark, is the lesson that the leaders in God's work need to learn. Heaven will not fail them in their day of adversity. Nothing is apparently more helpless, yet really more invincible, than the soul that feels its nothingness, and relies wholly on God.—*Prophets and Kings,* pp. 174, 175.

Selected Bibliography

Adams, Jay Edward. *Shepherding God's Flock: A Handbook on Pastoral Ministry, Counseling and Leadership.* 1986.

Anderson, Leith, et al. *Who's in Charge? Standing Up to Leadership Pressures* (Mastering Ministry's Pressure Points). 1993.

Anderson, Lynn. *They Smell Like Sheep: Biblical Leadership for the 21st Century.* 1997.

Armour, Michael C., and Don Browning. *Systems-sensitive Leadership: Empowering Diversity Without Polarizing the Church.* 1997.

Banks, William L. *The Black Church in the U.S.: Its Origin, Growth, Contributions, and Outlook.* 1972.

Barna, George, ed. *A Fish Out of Water.* 2002.

————. *Leaders on Leadership: Wisdom, Advice, and Encouragement on the Art of Leading God's People* (Leading Edge Series). 1997.

Becker, Carol E. *Leading Women: How Church Women Can Avoid Leadership Traps and Negotiate the Gender Maze.* 1996.

Bennis, Warren. *On Becoming a Leader.* 2003.

Bennis, Warren, and Burt Nanous. *Leaders: The Strategies for Taking Charge.* 1985.

Berkley, James D. *Leadership Handbooks of Practical Theology, Volume 3: Leadership and Administration; Ambition and Contentment.* 1995.

Bernstine, Karen Jones, ed. *Church and Family Together: A Congregational Manual for Black Family Ministry.* 1992.

Blackaby, Henry and Richard. *Spiritual Leadership.* 2001.

Blanchard, Ken, and Marc Muchnick. *The Leadership Pill.* 2003.

———— and Phil Hodges. *The Servant Leader.* 2003.

Bolman, Lee, and Terrence Deal. *Reframing Organizations.* 2003.

Brister, C. W. *Pastoral Care in the Church.* 1992.

Brown, Daniel A., et al. *The Other Side of Pastoral Ministry: Using Process*

Leadership to Transform Your Church. 1996.

Burns, J. M. *Leadership.* 1978.

Burt, Steve. *Activating Leadership in the Small Church: Clergy and Laity Working Together* (Small Church in Action). 1987.

Callahan, Kennon L. *Effective Church Leadership: Building on the Twelve Keys.* 1997.

Carroll, Jackson W. *As One With Authority: Reflective Leadership in Ministry.* 1991.

Cottrell, D., and E. Harvey. *Leadership Courage.* 2004.

Covey, S. *The Courage to Change: Living the 7 Habits.* 1999.

———. *The Eighth Habit—From Effectiveness to Greatness.* 2004.

———. *Principle-centered Leadership.* 1991.

Cueni, Robert R. *The Vital Church Leader* (Effective Church Series). 1991.

Dale, Robert D. *Leading Edge: Leadership Strategies From the New Testament.* 1996.

Day, Dan. *A Guide to Marketing Adventism.* 1990.

Drucker, P. *The Effective Executive.* 1985.

———. *Managing the Nonprofit Organization.* 1992.

Dudley, Roger, and Des Cummings. *Adventures in Church Growth.* 1983.

Engstrom, Ted W., and David J. Juroe. *The Making of a Christian Leader.* 1978.

Finzel, Hans. *The Top Ten Mistakes Leaders Make.* 1994.

Fisher, R., and W. Ury. *Getting to Yes.* 1981.

Ford, Leighton. *Transforming Leadership.* 1991.

Franklin, Robert. *Another Day's Journey.* 1997.

Freedman, S. *Upon This Rock.* 1993.

Gangel, Kenneth O. *Team Leadership in Christian Ministry: Using Multiple Gifts to Build a Unified Vision.* 1997.

Giuliani, Rudolph. *Leadership.* 2002.

Gladwell, Malcolm. *The Tipping Point.* 2002.

Goodman, Thomas. *The International Minister: 4 Powerful Steps to Determining, Implementing, and Fulfilling Your Ministry Priorities.* 1994.

Greenleaf, Robert K. *Servant Leadership.* 1977.

Haggard, Ted, and Lance R. Coles. *How to Run a Life-giving Church.* 1997.

Hanchey, Howard. *From Survival to Celebration: Leadership for the Confident Church.* 1994.

Harbaugh, Gary. *Pastor as Person.* 1984.

Harris, James H. *Pastoral Theology: A Black-Church Perspective.* 1991.

Harvey, James E. *Who's in Charge? Leadership Skills for Clergy and Others in Ministry*. 1996.

Hayford, Jack W. *Pastors of Promise: Pointing to Character and Hope as the Keys to Fruitful Shepherding* (Hayford Pastors Series). 1997.

Hemphill, Ken. *The Antioch Effect: 8 Characteristics of Highly Effective Churches*. 1994.

Hesselbein, F., M. Goldsmith, and R. Beckhard, *The Leader of the Future*. 1996.

Hollander, E. P. *Leadership Dynamics*. 1978.

House, Wayne H. *The Role of Women in Ministry Today*. 1995.

Johnson, Douglas W. *Don't Know Much About Being a Leader in My Church*. 1996.

Jones, L. *Jesus, CEO*. 1995.

Kallestad, Walt. *The Everyday, Anytime Guide to Christian Leadership*. 1994.

Knight, G. *If I Were the Devil*. 2007.

———. *Organizing to Beat the Devil*. 2001.

Kotter, John P. *A Force for Change*. 1990.

———. *Leading Change*. 1996.

Lee, Harris. *Effective Church Leadership*. 1990.

Lewis, Douglas G. *Meeting the Moment: Leadership and Well-being in Ministry*. 1997.

Lindgren, A., and N. Shawchuck. *Management for Your Church*. 1984.

Logan, Robert, and Carl F. George. *Leading and Managing Your Church*. 1988.

Longenecker, Harold. *Growing Leaders by Design: How to Use Biblical Principles for Leadership Development* (Country Shepherds Workshop Series). 1995.

Malphurs, Aubrey. *Values-driven Leadership: Discovering and Developing Your Core Values for Ministry*. 1996.

Maxwell, J. *Developing the Leaders Around You*. 1995.

———. *Developing the Leader Within You*. 1993.

———. *The Maxwell Leadership Bible*. 2002.

———. *The 21 Irrefutable Laws of Leadership*. 1998.

McCray, Walter A. *Black Young Adults: How to Reach Them, What to Teach Them*. 1992.

McGavran, Donald A. *Understanding Church Growth*. 1980.

McGinn, Linda. *Resource Guide for Women's Ministries*. 1990.

McIntosh, Gary. *The Exodus Principle: A Five-Part Strategy to Free Your*

People for Ministry. 1995.

McIntosh, Gary, and Glen Martin. *The Issachar Factor: Understanding Trends That Confront Your Church and Designing a Strategy for Success*. 1994.

McKenzie, Vashti M. *Not Without a Struggle: Leadership Development for African-American Women in Ministry*. 1996.

Miller, Calvin. *The Empowered Leader: 10 Keys to Servant Leadership*. 1996.

Miller, Herb, ed. *Leadership Is the Key: Unlocking Your Effectiveness in Ministry* (Leadership Insight Series). 1997.

Nelson, Alan E., and Herb Miller, eds. *Leading Your Ministry: A Moment of Insight Is Worth a Lifetime of Experience* (Leadership Insights Series). 1996.

Newman, Susan D. *With Heart and Hand: The Black Church Working to Save Black Children*. 1995.

Patzer, J. *The Road Ahead*. 2003.

Peters, T. J., and R. H. Waterman. *In Search of Excellence*. 1982.

Phillips, D. *Martin Luther King on Leadership*. 1999.

Powers, Bruce, ed. *Church Administration Handbook*. Revised and updated. 1997.

Purvis, Sally B. *The Stained-Glass Ceiling: Churches and Their Women Pastors*. 1995.

Randall, Robert L. *The Time of Your Life: Self/Time Management for Pastors*. 1994.

Reddin, W. J. *Managerial Effectiveness*. 1970.

Richardson, Ronald W. *Creating a Healthier Church: Family Systems Theory, Leadership, and Congregational Life* (Creative Pastoral Care and Counseling Series). 1996.

Rock, C. *Church Leadership*. 1990.

Rusbuldt, Richard E. *Basic Leader Skills*. 1982.

Sanders, J. O. *Spiritual Leadership*. 1994.

Sanford, John A. *Ministry Burnout*. 1992.

Schaller, Lyle E. *Strategies for Change*. 1993.

Shapiro, Andrea. *Creating Contagious Commitment*. 2003.

Shawchuck, Norman, and Gustave J. Rath. *Benchmarks of Quality in the Church: 21 Ways to Continuously Improve the Content of Your Ministry*. 1994.

Shawchuck, Norman, and Roger Heuser. *Leading the Congregation: Caring for Yourself While Serving Others*. 1993.

Shupe, Anson D. *Wolves Within the Fold: Religious Leadership and Abuses of Power*. 1998.

Sims, B. J. *Servanthood*. 1997.

Smith, Donald P. *Empowering Ministry: Ways to Grow in Effectiveness*. 1996.

Stewart, C. F. *African-American Church Growth: 12 Principles of Prophetic Ministry*. 1994.

Swindoll, C. *Leadership*. 1983.

Stone, Sam E. *How to Be an Effective Church Leader*. 1997.

Thompson, James. *Equipped for Change: Studies in the Pastoral Epistles*. 1996.

Treston, Kevin. *Creative Christian Leadership: Skills for More Effective Ministry*. 1995.

Turner, Nathan W. *Leading Small Groups: Basic Skills for Church and Community Organization*. 1997.

Valley, C. A. "Managing Change in the Seventh-day Adventist Church: An Interpretative Study on the Establishment of the John Loughborough School." MBA dissertation, 1994.

———. "The Relationship of the Leader Behaviors of Pastors and Church Growth in the Lake Union Conference of Seventh-day Adventists." Doctoral dissertation, 1986.

Wagner, Peter. *Your Church Can Grow*. 2001.

Warren, R. *The Purpose-driven Church*. 1995.

Wheatley, M. *Leadership and the New Science*. 1999.

Weems, Lovett H., Jr. *Church Leadership: Vision, Team, Culture, and Integrity*. 1993.

Wills, Gary. *Certain Trumpets: The Call of Leaders*. 1994.

Wilson, Robert A., ed. *Character Above All*. 1995.

Wimberly, Edward. *African-American Pastoral Care*. 1991.